DANCING
T H E W H E E L

DANCING

THE *of* WHEEL

PSYCHOLOGICAL TYPES

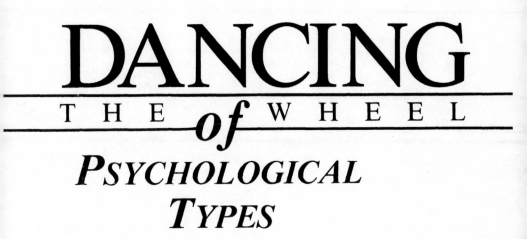

MARY E. LOOMIS

Chiron Publications • Wilmette, Illinois

Library of Congress Catalog Card Number: 90-25469

Printed in the United States of America.
Edited by Siobhan Drummond.
Book design by Elaine Hill.
Cover design by Michael Barron.
Cover photography by Kurt Hasselquist.

Library of Congress Cataloging-in-Publication Data:
Loomis, Mary, 1929 –
    Dancing the wheel of psychological types / Mary E. Loomis.
    p.   cm.
    Includes bibliographical references and index.
    ISBN 0-933029-49-7 : $14.95
    1. Typology (Psychology) 2. Individuation (Psychology)
  3. Medicine wheels. 4. Jung, C. G. (Carl Gustav), 1875-1961.
  5. Reagan, Harley Swiftdeer. I. Title.
  BF698.3.L66 1991
  158'.1 – dc20   90-25469
                                              CIP

ISBN 0-933029-49-7

To Bob, who dances in my heart

And to my children, Elizabeth, Robert, Barbara,
Margaret, Pamela, and Carrie,
who wondered what their mother was about

Contents

Introduction

"How can I change when I was born that way?" The question, almost a lament, was voiced by a man in his late thirties. He had telephoned me out of desperation, seeking help in disentangling himself from a web of complex relationships. He had been complaining about the women in his life, two ex-wives and a current ex-girl friend. He couldn't understand why they were acting the way they were. What was he to do? It wasn't his fault that he was in a mess. He was just a victim of circumstances. It was his fate. He wanted someone, anyone (in this instance, me) to tell him how to solve his problems, for he could see no way out. As I questioned him about his own behavior, implying that he had some responsibility for his predicament, he had replied with that lament.

Although this man asserted he was willing to do anything to solve his problems, what he actually meant was that he was willing to do anything except change himself. He could see where the women in his life needed to change but was unable to see how he contributed to his dilemma. Not only was he blind, he felt powerless to make any changes. The only solution he knew was to leave, and he had reached the point where there were no more places to go. Wouldn't someone else, please, take the responsibility for his life? He did not want it.

The world is full of people like this man, people who believe that if only the other person would change, everything would be just fine. This book is not for those people. This book is for the increasing number of individuals who know that change is possible and who recognize that any improvement in their lives has to begin with a change within themselves. This book is also for those individuals who don't know if they can change but who are willing to try.

There is no easy road to changing and transforming one's personality. It is a hard task but the rewards are great. If an individual is determined to awaken from the sleep of ages and take responsibility as a conscious human being for his or her own life, there is a way. What I offer in this book is one way the changes can begin. It is a path toward consciousness that combines certain ancient Native American teachings and contemporary Jungian psychology. It is a way that honors the spirit within each human being, the spirit that urges us toward wholeness. It is a way that I, as a Jungian analyst, have found to be rich and rewarding, albeit demanding, in my own life.

No two paths toward wholeness are identical. Each of us has to begin with where we are in our own life situation. Yet there are some similarities. Regardless of the path chosen, the first step requires that you determine where you are, that you recognize the patterns in your life — patterns of relationships, patterns of behaviors, patterns of beliefs, and patterns of thought. Only by recognizing the patterns can you identify where changes need to occur. In most cases the journey begins with a crisis. For it is only when we realize that something is wrong in our lives that we begin to search for ways to change. The crisis could be a loss of a job, a physical illness, an emotional distress, or an inner conflict. Few people are willing to make changes when everything in their lives seems to be going smoothly. There is no reason for them to change. If you are aware that you want to change, grow, expand, then this book may help your process.

The path I am proposing draws upon ancient Native American teachings: the medicine wheel, the Powers of the Four Directions, and the Star Maiden Circle. These were taught to me by Harley Swiftdeer, a Cherokee medicine man. This tradition is primarily Cherokee, but includes teachings from other matriarchal tribes such as the Navaho. I will use these teachings intermingled with Jungian psychology, particularly Jung's theory of psychological types, to compose a blueprint for a path toward wholeness, a path Jung referred to as the process of individuation and which the Native Americans refer to as the Red Road. The intention of this blueprint is to provide guideposts to help you determine where you are at this moment and to aid you in identifying where you need to change. The change does not always require that you discard old abilities, perceptions, and attitudes, but it does require that you expand your consciousness to include new abilities, perceptions, and attitudes. Sometimes the new supplants the old, but more often the new stands with the old so that your abilities, perceptions, and attitudes are expanded.

The dynamics of Jung's theory of psychological types utilized in this path is classical Jung. But it is not the commonly understood theory. Conceptually, I have adhered closely to Jung's writings. However, the theoretical formulation of how the functions are arranged in the psyche have been reformulated in accordance with empirical findings and the Native American teachings.

Anyone who is willing to examine himself or herself honestly can profit from this path. Sometimes an analyst or counselor is required to help us see our blocks, but for many, many individuals, self-examination reveals what has to be done. Self-healing is what this book is all about.

I offer the Native American teachings included in this book with the full approval of Harley Swiftdeer, the Cherokee medicine man who has been my teacher for several years. In the tradition of the Sacred Dream where the aim is to touch one's self, life, and others with beauty, half of the royalties of this book will go to the Deer Tribe Metis Medicine Society which Swiftdeer chiefs.

Chapter 1

The Medicine Wheel and the Powers
of the Four Directions

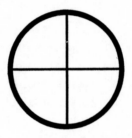

In the Native American tradition, the source of all creation is the Sacred Mystery, the Great Spirit. The Great Spirit is not the patriarchal God of the Judeo-Christian-Muslim tradition but a creative–conceptive force combining feminine and masculine potentials in harmonious balance. This Sacred Mystery reveals itself as the Powers of the Four Directions and these four powers provide the organizing principle for everything that exists in our world.

To gain self-awareness and enlightenment, one has to be in harmony with the Powers of the Four Directions and the source of all life. The medicine wheel, symbolized by a cross within a circle, provides a tool for achieving this balance and harmony. The medicine wheel is a ceremonial tool but it also provides the basis for all teaching wheels; the Powers of the Four Directions is implied, although not explicitly stated, whenever a wheel or a circle is drawn.

In the symbol of the medicine wheel, the Powers of the Four Directions are represented by the four cardinal points, that is, where the cross intersects the circle. The Power of the East is to the right, the Power of the West to the left. The Power of the

South is at the bottom of the circle, the Power of the North at the top. The circle around the cross is important for two reasons. First, the Native American perspective views life as a continuous cycle. Life, for them, mirrors the cycling of the seasons, the daily rising of the sun, and the phases of the moon. Life is not seen as linear with a beginning and an end, but viewed as spiraling ever onward in a sunwise, clockwise fashion. Jung shared this perspective, for he also described life as a continuing spiral. The second reason for the importance of the circle in the medicine wheel symbol is that the Native American view holds that all things — humans, rocks, stars, trees, animals — are interrelated. Separation is an illusion. The medicine wheel incorporates the Powers of the Four Directions and the cycling, interrelatedness of all things.

The teachings I have received from Swiftdeer were until recently an oral tradition. The teachings began with the drawing of a circle, and this simple form was overlaid with the elementary forces and expanded with the Powers of the Four Directions and their meaning for human beings. As he taught, I could imagine an elder drawing a circle in the earth and telling the story of the Powers of the Four Directions to a group of children gathered around him. With written material, the intimacy of an oral tradition is lost and a linearity is imposed upon the flowing, circular material. I will try to recreate the simplicity of Swiftdeer's teachings and hope to convey to you the elegance of this system.

Imagine a circle drawn in the earth or, if your imagination will not carry you back to those ancient times, imagine the circle being drawn on a sheet of newsprint held on an easel. Then imagine the gradual overlaying of symbols and meanings. The first symbols placed around the circle deal with the four elements: air, fire, water, and earth. This is the first manifestation of the Sacred Mystery in our physical reality. Air is in the north, fire in the east. Water is in the south and earth in the west. The wheel would look like this:

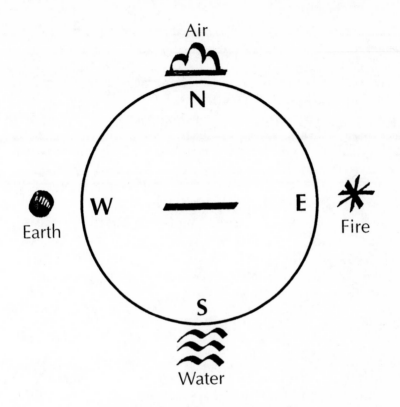

Figure 1. Medicine Wheel and the Elements

The center of the wheel represents the Sacred Mystery, the void that contains all potentials. Notice that the void, which can be represented by a zero, is not empty. It contains all things in a pre-nascent state. Jungians might view this as the realm of the collective unconscious or the realm of the archetypes.

The teaching would continue with an explanation of the four directions. The east is the place of the sun and has the color yellow. The west is the place of the earth and has the color black. The south is the place of the plant world and has the color red, while the north is the place of the animal world and has the color white.

The elder would explain that each direction has a specific relationship to energy. In the south, the energy flows just as water flows; it is the place of giving. In the west, the energy is held as the earth holds the energy upon which we stand. The north receives energy, and the east moves energy in a determined way. The center is the place of the catalytic energy.

Everything that exists can be organized according to the Powers of the Four Directions. Human races are organized with the red race placed in the south, the black race in the west, the white race in the north, and the yellow race in the east. The red race have been the givers to the human world, the black race the holders, the white race the receivers, and the yellow race the determiners. In the center would be the rainbow people, the people of mixed blood. Since all humans have red blood, black pupils, white bones, and yellow marrow, all humans could become catalytic energy for other humans if they would wake up and move from the place assigned to them by birth to another place on the circle and eventually into the center.

Each direction has a specific teaching for humans, and the elder would begin these teachings by explaining how the five human aspects are arranged on the wheel. Human emotions are placed in the south, the physical body in the west, the human mind in the north, the spirit in the east, and sexuality in the center.

For humans, the Power of the East, with the sun and fire, illuminates what is possible and sparks the imagination. There are lessons to learn from everything in the world and without light we cannot become enlightened. Since our spiritual aspect sits in the east and the east is the place of determining energy, it is with the spirit that we are to determine how our energy is to be spent.

The Power of the West with earth and blackness teaches us the value of introspection and how connection with the earth can lead to insight, finding the light within the dark and discovering the lessons of the world within. The west teaches us that we are to hold energy with our physical bodies, for our bodies are of the earth and connect us to the inner world. It is through the holding of energy that we can give form, give birth to new life.

The Power of the South, with the plants who give their lives that we may live, teaches us to be trusting and innocent, seeking perfection. It is the place where we are to learn the lesson of freely giving, flowing with our emotions.

The Power of the North, the place of the animals who instinctively live in harmony and balance, teaches us what perfection is. This is where we are taught to receive with our minds so that we may gain wisdom and logic.

Sexual energy, in the center of the wheel, is the catalytic energy connecting humans with the Sacred Mystery. The medicine wheel would now look like this:

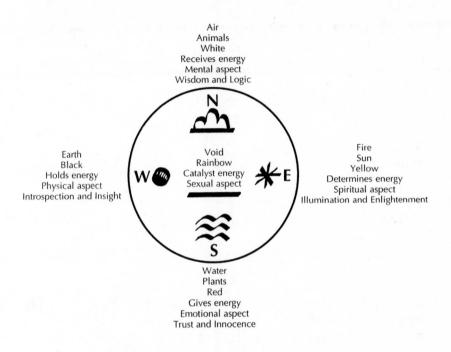

Figure 2. The Powers of the Four Directions

To align with the Powers of the Four Directions using this basic wheel requires that individuals examine their five human aspects, that is, the emotional, physical, mental, spiritual, and sexual components of their personalities, and question if the five aspects are in balance. Is the same amount of energy being spent in each aspect? Is there an aspect which is underdeveloped? Do I have my body in good shape? Am I in touch with my emotions? Am I sacrificing sexuality for spirituality? And further, are the five aspects aligned with the energy relationships appropriate to their directions on the wheel? Each person needs to ask: Am I giving with my emotions, holding with my physical body, receiving with my mind, and determining with my spirit? Is sexuality the catalytic energy of my being? Common

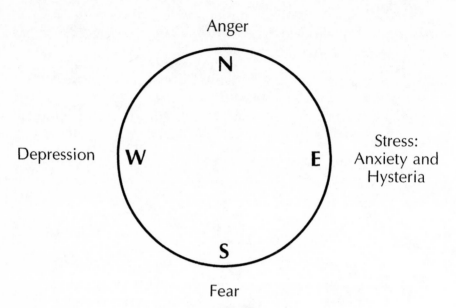

Figure 3. The Emotions Wheel

misalignments occur when we hold with our emotions, or when we determine, by prejudging, with our minds. Misalignments also occur when we give with our sexuality or give with our physical bodies.

This basic medicine wheel of the Powers of the Four Directions can be expanded to include other wheels so that there are wheels within wheels. Two of the wheels are relevant now. One is the emotions wheel and the other is the mind wheel. The emotions wheel is in the south of the basic medicine wheel, the mind wheel in the north. The emotions wheel depicts those emotions that impede your personal growth.

On the emotions wheel, fear is in the south, depression in the west, anger in the north, and stress—both anxiety and hysteria—in the east. The emotions wheel is a diagnostic aid analyzing where misalignments are occurring. It can be entered at any point. For example, if you are suffering from depression, you would note that depression is in the west of the wheel. On all medicine wheels, the west is the place of introspection and insight. This suggests there is a misalignment with the Power of the West, with your ability to be introspective, that there is a resistance to going within to find the inner truth. I will return

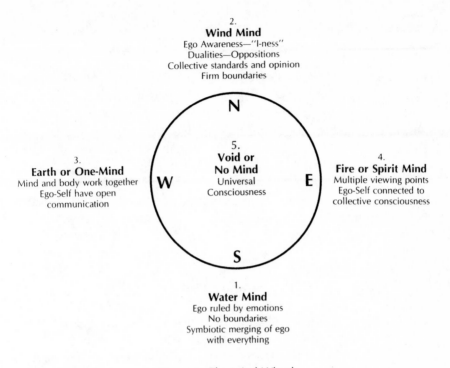

Figure 4. The Mind Wheel

to the emotions wheel shortly, but at this point I want merely to illustrate the organizing power offered by the Powers of the Four Directions.

The second wheel that is relevant for this material is the mind wheel, and it differs from the emotions wheel in that everyone enters the mind wheel from the south. Where the emotions wheel is a diagnostic wheel, the mind wheel is a developmental wheel. It depicts the process toward wholeness, or what Jungians would call the process toward being an individuated personality. On the wheel, the progression begins in the south and then moves north, west, east, and finally to the center.

The south of the mind wheel is the place of the water mind. It is a mind guided by emotions. This is the child mind with the rapid shifting from happiness to sadness to anger or to depression. In adults with a water mind, there is a continual inner dialogue which the individual cannot silence; there is no separation between the individual and the influences of the inner dialogue.

The north of the mind wheel is the place of the wind mind. It is the adult mind with intermittent inner dialogue. It is the mind of dualities. The person here separates the world into opposites and categorizes everything in order to understand. There is a separation of good from bad, right from wrong. For the person with a wind mind, the world is composed of opposites and oppositions. Self-awareness has begun but there is a strong reliance on collective values and approved behaviors. The person is aware of instincts and the need to control them. In Freudian terms, the person experiences the conflict of id and superego. In Jungian terms, the person has an awareness of unconscious processes yet has not integrated them.

The movement from the water mind of the child to the wind mind of the adult is the natural progression for human beings. However, there is no prescribed length of time for moving from one developmental mind stage to another. There is not an automatic correspondence with one's chronological age. Some people never leave the water mind and others, because of life situations, move into the adult wind mind at an early age.

When an individual begins the difficult process of dissolving the opposites, the developmental process moves her or him toward the west to earth mind. This is where mental processes and bodily knowing merge to form one-mind. Separations no longer exist. Opposites are viewed as mirror images of each other with equal value assigned to both. Earth mind is a disciplined mind where conscious and unconscious components of the person's personality are in harmony. The inner dialogue of the ego is replaced by the open communication between one's lower self and one's higher self. This is not the continual chatter of the water mind, but a harmonious working together of mind and body, with bodily knowledge incorporated into the mind. An example of one-mind would be those martial arts masters whose training includes Zen or another religious tradition. They are the ones who, although blindfolded and spun around, can hit the bull's eye of a target. Needless to say, the state of one-mind only results after years of discipline and hard work. Very few humans so far have attained it.

The fourth stage is the fire mind in the east. The fire mind is also called spirit mind. This mind is capable of holding multiple viewpoints. The sense of self exists but the ego is capable of suspending its particular viewpoint. The fire mind is also referred to as clear mind or mirror mind. Where few people ever attain one-mind in the west of the wheel, fewer still move to the point of having a fire mind. That point, in the east of the wheel, would be held by the enlightened ones, those beings like Jesus or Buddha who walked the world in human form and were connected to the universal consciousness.

The final stage of mental development for humans is represented by the center of the circle. This is the place of the void, or no-mind. It is here where all things are possible. Here the individual's connection to the Sacred Mystery is complete.

The teachings of the emotions wheel and the mind wheel demonstrate a way of looking at the human personality which makes sense to me. Although emotions and mind are different aspects of human beings and often in opposition, they are related to each other. The medicine wheel illustrates this relationship. Emotions are placed in the south and the mind in the north, diametrically opposed on the wheel. Yet they are interconnected, they are both on the circle. Individuals following the Red Road, the path toward individuation, are required to unite the emotions and the mind. It is not a matter of either one or the other but a synthesis of the two, symbolized by a bridge from the south to the north on the medicine wheel. Conscious individuals, according to this system, would be those who could give freely with their emotions; childlike, they could cry when sad and laugh when happy; and at the same time, these individuals could use their minds in a wise, nonprejudicial way. Admittedly, this is a difficult task.

Bridging the medicine wheel from south to north is one way of dancing the wheel. Bridging the wheel between east and west is another. An east–west bridge would bring spirit into substance (east to west) or substance into spirit (west to east). The east with Grandfather Sun is masculine energy. The west, the place of Grandmother Earth, is feminine energy. In this system, creation results when form is given to the image, when the spirit is made flesh, or when an idea is birthed, as in writing a book.

Dancing a wheel, whether the dance is circular or bridging, is a process of gaining self-awareness. Not all wheels are for dancing. Some, for example, the emotions wheel, are diagnostic, and although they aid in self-awareness, one would not be encouraged to move from anger to stress to fear to depression in a cycling dance. Rather, one would look at these impediments to wholeness (and that is what these four emotions are) and see how they relate to other aspects of the basic wheel. These emotions indicate a misalignment with the Powers of the Four Directions. As I mentioned earlier, depression is connected to the body and the holding of energy. A resolution of depression requires that one go within, sink into the depression. Usually persons with depression resist experiencing the inner world; their minds are racing, and they resist suspending their mental activities. They do not want to surrender control by quieting their mind and going into their bodies. But depression is just that. The energy is flowing inward. A resolution of the depression requires introspection, meditation, and mental stillness. It might be that the individual can dissolve the depression by sitting quietly for 10 or 15 minutes at a time, until the process of stopping the mental dialogue is learned.

Each of the emotional impediments has a teaching. Anger, connected to mental processes, indicates that the mind is not being used to receive information. How many times have you seen tempers flare over disagreements as to what is right? Often arguments in a family occur because the child has ideas different from the parent. When anger occurs, there is holding or closing of the mind and a lack of wisdom. There may be control issues involved, with one person trying to get another to submit to his or her beliefs or standards. Resolution of anger requires accepting another's point of view as valid.

Stress, in the east, is related to imagination and illumination. Something is awry in that connection. If you question hysterics or anxiety-ridden people as to what they imagine as possibilities for themselves, you will find that often they are limited to an either–or mentality. They have difficulty imagining three or four alternatives to problems in their lives. Opening their imagination is the solution.

Fear, in the south, is the most pervasive of all the negative emotions. It is usually the first block to selfhood that a child encounters. And it is fear that often prevents you from being open with your emotions. Recognizing and confronting one's fears is the only way to dissolve them.

Notice that sadness and happiness, crying and laughing, are not on the emotions wheel. Crying when one is sad, laughing when one is happy indicates a harmony between what is experienced and what is expressed. Being in the moment, not denying or suppressing, would be the natural, healthy way to be giving and flowing with your emotions. This would be the proper alignment with the Power of the South. Laughing and crying when they are appropriate are not impediments to increased consciousness.

All medicine wheels are tools for understanding our humanity. Some are teaching wheels, explaining where human beings fit into the grand scheme of the universe. Others are working wheels, pointing out what it means to be human. Being human is differentiated from being a two-legged animal in these teachings. Being human means being conscious and being responsible for one's self-growth. These Native American teachings of the Red Road, the path to wholeness, are compatible with the tenets of Jungian psychology and the individuation process. This book, while not a wheel, will dance back and forth between these Native American teachings and Jungian psychology, using one to illuminate the other.

Chapter 2

*Persona, Shadow, Ego, Self, and the
Transcendent Function*

The Jungian Process of Individuation

In the psychology of Carl Jung, the movement toward wholeness, toward increased consciousness, is called the process of
individuation. It is a process that has as its aim the realization,
or actualization, of an individual's unique personality. Individuation proceeds through the resolution of conflicts, conflicts
that are caused by a one-sidedness in our perceptions, attitudes, beliefs, and behaviors. These conflicts, which may be
mild or extreme, cause emotional or physical distress and sig-
nal where we are blocked and prevented from becoming the
persons we were meant to be.

Individuation begins with an examination of one's personal
history and a healing of the wounds of childhood. But the process does not stay in the past. It is vitally concerned with the
present and the future. Individuals who embark on this path
toward increased consciousness become aware of, and listen
to, the promptings of a higher power operating in their lives.
This does not mean surrendering completely to the promptings
of the higher power, for this would mean a surrendering of free
will and a loss of individual responsibility. The process of individuation requires that you maintain your own sense of identity and that you willingly engage the process, accepting
responsibility for who you are. It is like a dance. You move to
engage the various aspects of your personality and as you
dance, the conscious and unconscious aspects of your personality align in harmonious balance.

Jung went to great pains to define individuation. He stated
that it is not individualism, or a selfish egocentrism, but a
union of the diverse parts of the personality resulting in an

indivisible unit which is nothing less than the unique personality of a human being, aware of, listening to, and learning from the unconscious influences operating in her or his life. A paradoxical situation evolves when human beings begin this individuation process. As they focus on their inner work and conflicts are gradually resolved, these individuals, instead of becoming separated or alienated from the rest of humanity, discover a common bond linking them to all human beings. Each person they meet becomes a mirror for them, and each human interaction, each relationship, becomes an opportunity for personal growth. Individuals on this path begin recognizing parts of themselves in every person they encounter. Some parts are liked and some parts are disliked. But it is a fact that without other people and the mirroring we do for each other, individuation is impossible.

Jung used several concepts in explaining the individuation process. Among them are persona, shadow, ego, and Self. He also used other concepts and terms such as the transcendent function and projection. To understand these terms and concepts and to see how they are interrelated, it is helpful to examine how a personality develops.

Somewhere in childhood, early in our personal history, we develop an ego. We have likes and dislikes. We become aware of a sense of "I-ness." Even a small toddler can say "Me want" with conviction and intensity. This ego, the place of I, is the center of one's will, and it is the starting place of the individuation process, for without an ego there is no consciousness. Out of our experiences, we develop an ego ideal which represents how we want to be and how we want to be seen by others. Usually our ego ideal has to do with our strivings to be seen and appreciated by our parents, in which case we may adopt a stance that we know they will approve. We may become the dutiful daughter, the scholar-athlete, or the independent child. Or we may decide, in order to get attention, to reject the standards and behaviors of our parents. It is not uncommon for adults to recall a decision, made in childhood, when they swore they would never be like their parents. They remember thinking: "When I grow up, I won't treat my children like that."

All of us make a decision in childhood which shapes the way we view ourselves and how we behave with other people. We may not be able to remember clearly just when that decision was made, but however it occurs, an ego ideal takes form. This ego ideal becomes the cornerstone of our persona. It is the embodiment of how we want to be seen by other people. Any behaviors, attitudes, or thoughts which do not conform to our ideal image of ourselves are repressed, suppressed, forgotten, or denied. But these behaviors, attitudes, and thoughts do not disappear. They stand behind us in our shadow, seen by others who know us, but unseen and unadmitted by us. The more we strive for what we consider to be perfection, that is, for attaining our ego ideal, the more our ego is identified with our persona and the darker our shadow becomes. The development of persona and shadow is a natural process. Without a persona, anchored by an ego ideal, we would not have survived childhood. It was essential that we chose to be a certain way and turned our backs on other alternatives; the choosing allowed the ego to develop and become strong.

Everything that is contrary to our ego ideal, everything that we designate as inferior, undesirable, or unwanted, falls into our shadow. For example, if I have an ego ideal that says I will not be critical, that I will always strive to look on the bright side and to be loving and supportive of those around me, I am relegating to my shadow my critical judging faculties. With my emphasis on staying on the bright, positive side, being eternally optimistic, I am denying disagreeable realities which I refuse to see or acknowledge. I say "Get thee behind me" to everything that does not conform to my ego ideal. I maintain my loving, supportive posture even though it is stifling me. I subjugate myself, martyrlike, for the benefit of others. In my heart of hearts, I know what I am doing. I have made a decision to be a certain way. Of course, the decision could have been made so early and be such an integral, habitual part of my personality that I cannot imagine being any other way.

As I mature, my ego ideal becomes the major component of my persona. It is the way I want to be seen. If someone confronts me, stating that I am unkind, unloving, or unsupportive, I feel unjustly criticized. I deny I am that way. Can't they see how loving and supportive I am? I may become angry because my feelings are hurt. I cannot admit to myself or to others that I have a negative critical side within me. I am defensive because someone has seen my shadow. I don't want anyone to see my dark side, and I certainly don't want to look at it myself.

Although developmentally, we need to defend our egos in order to survive childhood with some sense of our own being, our own will power, in adulthood those ego defenses we utilized as children become maladaptive. In growing up, striving toward our ego ideals, we relegate so much of ourselves to our shadows that we need to expend increasing amounts of energy to keep our shadows at bay. If we were to assimilate the contents of our shadows, we would have to change our ego ideals and that terrifies us. We have survived so far, why change?

The shadow, containing all that we experienced in our lives which conflicts with our ego ideal, is everything we cannot accept about ourselves at this present time or couldn't accept about ourselves in the past. The shadow also contains all those parts of our personality which we have ignored or failed to develop. Perhaps there is an artistic ability that had to be set aside in order to make our way in the world. We may have minimized or negated that ability because we could not develop that talent and hold our ego ideal at the same time. So this undeveloped talent, this potential gift, resides in our shadow along with all the other forgotten aspects of our potential wholeness. In addition to the personal elements from our history, there is also a collective aspect to the shadow. We may be holding societal, religious, or political values and, from this viewpoint, we may be rejecting unquestioningly whatever does not conform to the group's standards. Everything we reject from an individual or collective viewpoint lies in the shadow. The function of the shadow, its importance for psychological growth, is that the contents of the shadow balance the one-sidedness of our ego ideal.

Paradoxically, although the shadow contains all the personality elements that are considered negative and inferior by the ego, it is within these inferior contents of the shadow that the areas of future growth reside. From another person's viewpoint, the contents of one's shadow may not be seen as negative or inferior. It is in the shadow that the discarded stone lies, the stone that is to become the keystone for the mason in the parable of building the arch. It is in the dung heap of the shadow that the philosopher's stone is found, the stone that in alchemy signifies wholeness. The shadow, from the perspective of the ego ideal, appears dark and undesirable, its bright potential unseen. For an individual seeking increased consciousness, the shadow points out where the work is to be done.

While the shadow contains all that we want to hide, the persona is just the opposite. The persona contains all the aspects of our personality which we want to display to society. The persona is the mask we wear as we assume a social role. It signifies our part in the social drama. To say the persona is a mask tends to portray it as somehow false. Nothing could be further from the truth. Social roles with their personae are necessary for human interactions in community and society. Without designated roles, society could not function. For example, if you are taking a bus downtown for an important meeting, you have every right to expect that the bus driver will travel the prescribed route and deposit you at the destination you have selected. You might be more than irritated if the driver took a different route, or if the driver stopped in the middle of the road and began lecturing on nuclear physics. We expect a bus driver to drive a bus, a priest to provide spiritual guidance, a police officer to keep the peace. Society has a right to require each of us to fulfill our chosen roles. Without roles, there could be no society. Regardless of our position, we all wear a mask. We all fill a social role. We all have a persona.

Notice that the persona is a collective function. It is the role we play that is important for society, not the person in the role. The function of the role is what matters. The uniqueness of the the person is not considered. When one person leaves a position, another takes it up. A teacher retires, a new teacher is hired. It is as in the days of monarchies: when the ruler died, the cry went out, "The king is dead, long live the king," announcing an unbroken lineage. For such a society to endure, there always had to be someone on the throne. For our society, there must always be bus drivers, police officers, teachers, priests, and doctors, each doing what is expected of him or her.

A few people are born into their roles in society. Most gravitate to the role that fits their training and personality and ultimately their ego ideal. Jung said that the task of the first half of life is to adjust to the demands of society and that this adjustment is an important aspect of the individuation process. Some of us adjust to society through careers, others of us through families. If one has opted for motherhood, then the persona she wears is the mask of mother. Someone has to have the role of mother in society. The difficulty with persona arises when the fit is so complete that the individual becomes overidentified with the role and is not aware that the persona being worn is a mask.

Several years ago, I met a man who was an executive officer of a large corporation, one of the largest corporations in the country. He served in a volunteer capacity on several charity boards in the city and his name was frequently in the newspapers. As he neared retirement age, he anticipated donating more of his time and energy to these groups. When he finally retired, he was crestfallen to discover he was no longer wanted. He thought he, as an individual person, had been sought out by these groups when, in truth, the various boards wanted him for the prestige that his position could confer on their organizations. When he no longer had the title, he was no longer needed. This man had identified completely with his persona. His ego ideal and persona were merged. When he lost his social role, not knowing that there was more to his being than persona, a deep depression ensued.

Overidentification with one's persona is a major problem for people in the United States, since we often define ourselves and others by our professions or jobs. How many times have you asked or been asked by new acquaintances, "What do you do?" or "Where do you work?" As we identify people with their social role, we ignore the uniqueness of their being.

In the Jungian schema of the personality, the ego is the center of consciousness and of will. It is not the center of the human personality. The true center Jung called the Self with a capital "S." It could also be called one's inner higher self, or the inner image of wholeness. Theologians have called it the image of God within. This image of wholeness contains every possibility for human beings. The Self is not one-sided. In the Self, all oppositions are in balance. This is the force from within that urges us along on the path of individuation, calling us to be all that we can be. The Self is the center of the entire personality, encompassing both the conscious and the unconscious aspects. During the process of individuation, and often this does not occur until the second half of life, the individual recognizes that the ego is not the center of the personality. This recognition is akin to the earth discovering that it is not the center of the universe but is dependent upon the sun. The earth revolves around the sun in our solar system, not the other way around. When an individual recognizes that his or her ego is not the center of the personality, there is a major transformation within consciousness. The individual realizes how limited the ego really is. Although the ego is vital for consciousness, the individual begins to accept that there are forces beyond ego's control operating in her or his life. It is engaging in the dance between the ego and the Self that induces the individuation process to proceed. Whenever there is a conflict or a disruption in the normal course of events in one's life, the invitation to begin the dance is offered. The loss of a job, a physical illness, a mental distress are all invitations to begin the process of examining one's ego ideal, to determine where one-sidedness, embodied in our persona, has blocked the connection to the Self.

Dissolving our overidentification with our persona does not mean the destruction of the persona but it does mean a recognition that we are more than a social role. This almost always involves a reframing of our ego ideal; one of the first steps in the individuation process requires that we acknowledge that we are our shadow. This is hard, humbling work, and it takes conscious intent to pursue the goal of wholeness.

That which resides in our shadow, unconscious to our ego, becomes visible to us through a process called projection. We cannot grasp directly what is in our unconscious because, by definition, what is unconscious is unknown to consciousness. But we can see in others what we dislike in ourselves. We can also see in others strengths, abilities, and talents that we have not yet developed in ourselves. Our higher self projects these hidden aspects onto other people so we can learn the particular contents of our shadow which we need to assimilate. Our emotions provide the key to recognizing a projection, emotions that are sudden, intense, and extreme. If I have a strong, negative response to someone, the Self is calling me to examine myself to discover if I am seeing in that person certain traits or behaviors which I have judged undesirable and have excluded from my ego ideal. My higher self is telling me that now is the time to expand my conscious functioning. The negative emotional response was triggered because of the one-sided perspective of my persona, my ego ideal. As I identify the traits in the other person which I rejected and if I am honest with myself, I will be forced to admit that the traits in question do have a positive side which I had not seen before.

Once, at a meeting, I found myself becoming irritated with a colleague who had arrived late and then had persisted in discussing material which had been covered before his arrival. I became agitated, wishing I could gag him. In an outburst, I told him to stop it. I can't remember if I said "Shut up" or not, but it was pretty close to that. He was as shocked as I was with my behavior. Later, as I reflected on my emotional response and outburst, I realized that he embodied certain characteristics which I had excluded from the image I carried of myself. From the perspective of my persona and my ego ideal, the process of the group was of paramount importance. I remembered many times when I inconvenienced myself to further group harmony and admitted that frequently I harbored a residual resentment at my "self-sacrifice." My colleague, on the other hand, placed more importance on himself, on his wants and desires, than he did on group harmony. As I sat with this insight, I knew that my higher self was telling me, through the process of projection, that I was too one-sided, out of balance, with my ego ideal. It was time to change, to expand my perspective and values in regard to myself and groups. I acknowledged that there is a time to hold fast to your own values and desires even when the entire group disagrees with you. I admitted there was a positive side to my colleague's behavior. I could not admit this until after I had analyzed our interaction. Before this, I had thought him selfish, stubborn, and unconscious.

It is not always negative traits that are projected onto other people. If I am infatuated with someone, I am also being called by the Self to determine what unlived, highly regarded potentials I have not developed within my own being. What is it that I cannot see in myself but can only see in others? What am I giving over to someone else to carry for me?

A friend of mine once said that she constantly fell in love with college professors when she was a young woman. After she earned her own doctorate, her infatuation with professors ended. She had been projecting her own unlived, intellectual potential onto someone else. By developing her own intellectual capabilities, integrating into her conscious functioning what previously had been unrecognized in her own personality, the projections ceased.

Projection is an automatic process outside of ego control. It is one way that unconscious contents are made visible to us. Through the process of projection, other people become mirrors for us, reflecting back to us where we need to grow. Whenever we have an emotional response that is more extreme than the situation warrants, becoming angry or irritated with someone for just being who they are or becoming intrigued or infatuated with someone we hardly know, our emotions are telling us we are caught in a projection. It is a tip-off that we are seeing unconscious parts of our own personality. Individuation requires that we develop the unlived parts of our personality. Projections show us what those unlived parts are.

Becoming a whole person requires a commitment of our conscious will. We must be willing to recognize the unlived potential within us and determinedly address and integrate the neglected parts of our personality. This process of increasing our consciousness involves what Jung termed the *transcendent function*.

The term *transcendent function* can be misleading. It connotes for many of us something divine or otherworldly. But that is not how Jung defined the term. He defined it as being similar to what mathematicians mean when they use the term *transcendent function*, that is, a function which subsumes other functions. It is transcendent because it "facilitates a transition from one attitude to another" (Jung 1921, par. 828).

Jung said that, in dreams, a bridge often symbolized the transcendent function, and it was the bridging quality he wanted to convey by that term. Although it is a natural process, the transcendent function (in the process of individuation), which "allows the transition from one attitude to another without the loss of consciousness" (Jung 1958, par. 145) is earned through hard work. There is no divine intervention or *deus ex machina* to come with a miracle or wave of the wand to accomplish this task. It is arduous work. In the course of individuation, wherever we have a one-sided position, we are called to consciously, willfully attend to the opposite position. The transcendent function is "born of the union of opposites" (Jung 1928, par. 368). The conjoining of opposites is "a living birth that leads to a new level of being, a new situation" (Jung 1958, par. 189). The birthing of the transcendent function can be as laborious as the birthing of a human baby. It is not easy work.

The movement toward wholeness, toward increased consciousness, is a continually cycling process. "There is no change that is unconditionally valid over a long period of time. Life has always to be tackled anew" (Jung 1958, par. 142). The movement involving the transcendent function is a process we could liken to thesis, antithesis, synthesis (with the thesis representing our conscious one-sidedness, the antithesis the opposite, shadow quality we need to develop, and the synthesis the transcendent function joining the two). Synthesis then becomes the new thesis for the process to spiral onward.

The situation involved here is that one's will is an essential ingredient in determining to attend and consciously give energy to the unlived side. Then, paradoxically, the will must be suspended when the tension of opposites ensues. There must be a willingness to engage the process and then a suspension of will once the process is begun. For to give preference to one side or the other aborts the birth of the transcendent function. One has to be willing not to slip back into old familiar patterns, be willing to feel uncomfortable with the raw new attitudes or behaviors. Further, this process cannot occur if it is only imaged or intellectually considered. Life must be lived. In the process of my interactions with a group, for example, I had to begin valuing myself, holding, withstanding the feeling of being selfish, knowing that that would be the way some people would see me. As Jung said:

> The way of the transcendent function is an individual destiny. But on no account should one imagine that this way is equivalent to the life of a psychic anchorite, to alienation from the world. Quite the contrary, for such a way is possible and profitable only when the specific worldly tasks which these individuals set themselves are carried out in reality. (1928, par. 369)

The dance between the ego and the Self demands that we live life and engage in relationships with others. Without others, we cannot see our shadow, we cannot see what we have neglected or ignored. In other words, you cannot individuate on a mountain top. The process of individuation and the transcendent function results in an expansion of our ego ideal.

With each new union of conscious and unconscious contents, we gain freedom from a one-sided position and establish a broader base for our behaviors and attitudes. No longer will we automatically, habitually react with old behavior patterns. Now we can move consciously, meaningfully from our own center of being. As we alter our one-sided perspective to include other viewpoints, we move to a new level of being with a broader awareness of who we are.

"But how," you may ask, "does this process occur? What are the dynamics?" To answer these questions, let's examine how Jung envisioned the human mind functioning and what he saw as the practical psychology of the individuation process.

Chapter 3

Jung's Theory of Psychological Types

Practical Psychology

How we act, that is, how we behave and interact with the people around us, is influenced by a complex variety of factors. Not the least of these factors is our inner mental understanding of who we are. Most of us give little thought to how we view ourselves and even less to how we process information in order to make sense out of what is happening around us. We usually assume that the way we perceive the world is much the same as the way everyone else perceives the world. Nothing could be further from the truth. There are differences, sometimes dramatic differences, in how people perceive and interpret the world, and these differences lead to differences in behavior. For example, some people require organization and planning in living their lives. Others find planning and organization restrictive and live their lives "going with the flow" of what life offers.

If we want to grow in self-awareness, we need to understand how we have been perceiving the world and making sense out of our perceptions. We need to see how our perception of the world, our frame of reference, is different from the perceptions of others around us.

One of the tools for understanding individual differences is provided by Jung's theory of psychological types. It is a theory he developed from observing human nature. This theory offers us a key to understanding how we are functioning and provides a blueprint for the individuation process. It also helps us improve our communication with other individuals.

The first personality dimension that Jung described, and the one which formed a cornerstone for his theory of psychological types, was that of introversion–extraversion. This dimension emerged from his observation of the feud between Freud and Adler and his attempt to understand why these two men were unable to validate each other's perceptions and theories. Jung labeled Freud the extravert and Adler the introvert. Jung stated that human beings had a preferred attitude, either introverted or extraverted, which colored most of their actions, thoughts, and values. This preferred attitude or orientation is automatic and, according to Jung, is part of one's biological inheritance. The extravert's primary focus is on the outer, physical world. The introvert's primary focus is on the inner, psychological world.

Jung recognized that although the potential for both orientations exists in each individual, one or the other tends to predominate. As Jung described the behaviors connected with introversion and extraversion, he admitted that he was describing cases of extreme one-sidedness. But it was an exaggeration necessary to clarify his concepts. He knew that most individuals could be introverted in some situations and extraverted in others and that it would be an unusual person who has the adaptation of always being introverted or of always being extraverted.

Introverted individuals, Jung stated, would be focusing primarily on their inner, subjective world. What they experience, personally, is more important to them than what is happening in their outer surroundings. These people are energized by their inner world. This may be a world of ideas or visions. It may be a world of meditation which engages them or reflections on values such as sisterhood, freedom, or independence. As a rule, introverts are not concerned with how their thoughts and ideas are received by the outer world. Theirs is the world of "art for art's sake" or "knowledge for the sake of knowledge." Their voice may be that of the prophet crying in the wilderness. Introverts are comfortable by themselves. In an extremely introverted personality, there may be little or no regard given to the demands of the outer world whether the demands are placed by friends, family, or society.

In contrast, extraverted individuals attend primarily to the outer, physical world. It may be the world of human relationships, of family, friends, or pets. The physical environment with its colors, textures, and sounds, as well as career and achievement, are important to them. They may be engaged in finding solutions to problems in the business, social, or political realms, or imagining what may be possible in the world of tomorrow. Extraverts are energized by people, by the color of a rose, or the bustle of a city. When their extraversion is extreme, extraverts run the risk of losing their own sense of identity. If they have identified themselves with a job or a position, the loss of that job could be disastrous. Extraverts usually have many friends and acquaintances. In fact, they usually prefer doing things with another person or group of people rather than by themselves.

Jung's concept of introversion–extraversion is respected as a seminal dimension in personality theory (Maddi 1976). It has been incorporated into most personality inventories and questionnaires. The words themselves are now common in our everyday language, and we label this person an introvert and that person an extravert. However, the personality research on introversion and extraversion supports Jung's assertion that both orientations exist in each individual. Most people have flexibility in their orientations. They are not locked into always being introverted or always being extraverted. Some researchers have proposed the term *ambivert* to describe the great number of people who fall between the introverted and extraverted poles on personality questionnaires. Although the term *ambivert* begins to recognize the complexity of human functioning, it is too global. It does not clarify in what ways a person is introverted or in what ways a person is extraverted.

In Jung's original formulation of his theory, he hypothesized that the opposite orientation would emerge from the unconscious when the individual was unaware. Thus, if the person was predominately extraverted, the introverted side would come out at unexpected times, when the person was not paying attention to what was happening, or, as psychologists would say, times when ego control was diminished. The less-utilized orientation does not disappear from the personality. It is always present but not always seen or acknowledged. Jung's observation gives clues as to when introversion and extraversion occur, but this is not specific enough to be helpful to individuals moving toward increased consciousness. However, as we shall see, there is more to Jung's theory of psychological types than introversion and extraversion.

Jung stated that in addition to having a biologically derived preference for introversion or extraversion, human beings have four psychological functions inherent in their psychological makeup. Just as human beings each have two eyes, two ears, one head, etc., as part of their physical endowment, human beings also have four psychological functions that enable them to interact with, comprehend, and understand their environment. The environment may be the inner, personal world, in which case, the psychological functions would be utilized in an introverted adaptation. Or, if the environment in question is the outer, physical world, then the psychological functions would be utilized in an extraverted adaptation. Jung stressed that all four functions exist in each person but they are not equally well developed or utilized.

The four functions, as Jung defined them, are sensation, intuition, thinking, and feeling. As Jung described the four functions, he labeled two of them perceptual functions and two of them judging functions. Sensation and intuition comprise the perceiving pair. Thinking and feeling the rational, judging pair.

Sensation involves seeing, smelling, tasting, touching. It also involves kinesthetic, bodily awareness. Intuition, which Jung called perception via the unconscious, allows us to image what is possible by using our imagination. It is also the function that can encompass multiple viewpoints. While both sensation and intuition are perceiving functions, they are very different from one another. Sensation is connected to what exists in the present. It is a reality factor. Intuition allows us to transcend the present time and move into the future or into the past, encompassing the realm of possibilities.

In describing the judging functions, Jung described thinking as a logical thought process entailing cause-and-effect reasoning. He described feeling not as emotions, but as a process of value judgments. Jung labeled both thinking and feeling rational functions since both resulted in judgments. Both thinking and feeling are predictable methods people use to make decisions in their lives.

As Jung envisioned the interaction of the four functions, he saw them arranged as two pairs of opposites. Thinking and feeling, the rational functions, were opposed, as were sensation and intuition, the perceptual functions. To convey how he saw them working together, Jung offered the image of a cross.

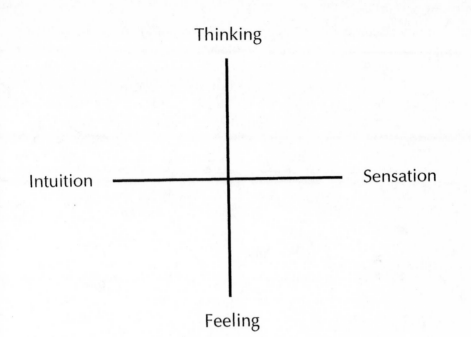

Figure 5. *Jung's Arrangement of the Four Functions*

According to this model, interactions could occur between adjacent functions, but not between opposing functions. This meant that interactions would always include a perceiving function and a judging function. Further, whatever function was the most highly developed would be opposite the function which was the least developed. For example, if thinking were the most highly developed function within one's personality, feeling would automatically be the least developed. Thinking, then, would be the superior function, feeling the inferior one. In this oppositional, cross arrangement, a superior function could have an adjacent function as an auxiliary. So that thinking, in this example, could be combined with intuition or with sensation in one's conscious orientation, but never with feeling. The undeveloped function, or functions, would remain in a primitive, undifferentiated state and would not be under the individual's conscious control.

The particular development of the four functions is something most of us have never thought about. But the truth is, we use the functions we are successful with and we do not use the undeveloped functions because we cannot rely on them. We develop patterns of habitual behavior, and we are not aware of the patterns.

This doesn't mean that the unused functions cease to exist; they just are not developed enough to be reliable. Each of us has the potential for the two orientations and four functions to be well developed in our personalities. But this possibility is not shown in the cross image. Let's step back and take a different perspective on Jung's theory of psychological types.

Jungian psychology is predicated on the idea of expanding one's consciousness. This process, the process of individuation, requires the resolution of opposites in one's personality. Jung, in fact, saw typology as providing a road map for the individuation process (Meier 1971). This observation is underscored by the complete title of the first English translation of his work on typology, *Psychological Types: The Process of Individuation* (Jung 1921). In this volume of the collected works, there is a lecture in which Jung stated that all four functions operating in balance were needed in order to be a fully functioning human being:

> These four basic functions seem to me sufficient to express and represent the various modes of conscious orientation. For complete orientation all four functions should contribute equally: thinking should facilitate cognition and judgment, feeling should tell us how and to what extent a thing is important or unimportant to us, sensation should convey concrete reality to us through seeing, hearing, tasting, etc., and intuition should enable us to divine the hidden possibilities in the background. (1921, par. 518)

The description Jung provides in the above paragraph seems to refer to the extraverted orientation of the functions, but that does not detract from his statement that all four functions are required. Because Jung hypothesized an opposition between sensation and intuition and between thinking and feeling, saying if one of the pair were the most highly developed, the opposite function would be the least developed, many students of his theory have overlooked Jung's statement that all four functions are needed for wholeness. Instead of seeing typology as a dynamic process, they see typology as a static system, providing categories for typing people. When they use typology in this manner, they are working contrary to Jung's intentions.

Jung refused to categorize people by type. In the Tavistock lectures, he said: "Do not think I am putting people into this box or that and saying, 'He is an intuitive,' or 'He is a thinking type' . . . . It is no use at all putting people into drawers with different labels" (Jung 1935, par. 34). He then goes on to say that when he does categorize behavior, it is for reasons of practical psychology, that is, for explaining the behaviors of one person to another, a husband to a wife, for example. Practical psychology requires simplifying a process to promote understanding. It is like stopping a frame in a motion picture so that it can be examined and analyzed.

The oppositional arrangement of the functions as imaged by the cross was a teaching device used by Jung to explain the possible interactions of the functions. Unfortunately, it has contributed to the misunderstanding of Jung's theory. The cross is an incomplete symbol. The oppositional arrangement contradicts Jung's basic premise that the aim of psychological growth is the resolution of opposites. But Jung's use of the cross symbol is not the only reason why misconceptions about his theory have occurred.

Jung was a scientist, and he detailed the results of his observations as he discovered them, hypothesizing future possibilities from the results at hand. If later observations proved his hypotheses incorrect, he modified his position. If you read his writings chronologically, you can see the evolution of his ideas. But that is a laborious process, for Jung's writings span more than half a century of psychological research. For example, in regard to typology, Jung did not stop writing about typology after his major work was published in 1921. However, his later comments and reflections are not neatly found in one volume. They are tucked away in footnotes, in letters to friends, in lectures, and in answers to seminar questions. It is in these later writings that Jung's intentions about typology become clear.

It is my intent in this book to clarify the concepts in Jung's theory of psychological types, utilizing his later, more obscure writings and comments. Then I will reframe the dynamics of his theory, from the vantage point of the Native American medicine wheel, in order to return to Jung's original intention that typology be a road map for the individuation process. The descriptions of the functions offered now will be brief. More complete descriptions of how typology works in individual personalities can be found in Chapter 7.

Most people have no difficulty in understanding sensation. It is the most basic of the four psychological functions. Sensation is the only function that can work by itself. It is through sensation that we gather the primary data from our inner and outer worlds. Sensation allows us to see, hear, smell, taste, and touch. It is through the kinesthetic sensations of our body that we know if we are stressed or relaxed. Sensation connects to the here and now. It allows us to note differences without prioritizing or valuing one thing over another. Sensation is a perceiving function.

Intuition is the second perceiving function. Intuition is the function of our imagination. We use intuition when we envision future possibilities or when we take another's viewpoint. Intuition allows us to perceive the overall picture without focusing on the details. It is the function most closely allied with our creative potential. When Jung called intuition "perception via the unconscious," he was trying to differentiate intuition from sensory perceptions. Intuition takes us beyond what exists in the present reality.

Both sensation and intuition provide us with information. Sensation gives us the details and the fine discriminations, intuition provides us with the overall effect or completed image of future possibilities.

The remaining two functions, thinking and feeling, are the judging functions. They organize the perceptual information we receive into understandable units. Thinking and feeling structure our worlds by prioritizing and categorizing into hierarchical systems which are sensible and reasonable to us. Both thinking and feeling measure, judge, and compare. They are the methods we use to reach decisions.

Thinking is a logical thought process, primarily involved in problem solving. When thinking is utilized, individuals proceed methodically, weighing alternatives for their relative strengths and weaknesses, and then selecting the option that provides the greatest positive outcome for the least cost. Thinking proceeds as a step-by-step process in reaching decisions, and most of us like to think that we are very logical in the decisions we make. In truth, most of our decisions are made through value judgments of what we like or dislike, utilizing the function that Jung labeled feeling (Zajonc 1980).

Feeling is a rational process of evaluation according to an inner, personal or an outer, shared standard of values. It is a predictable and consistent process, concerning what one likes and dislikes, what one holds dear and what one disdains. If you know what a person's values are, you can predict that person's behavior. Values are often not consciously known nor are we always able to articulate them, but there is a consistency to what we value. Often we hear people say something to the effect that: "I can't tell you what I like, but I know what I like when I see it." As Zajonc (1980) noted, we can be wrong about the decisions we reach through logical, methodical thought processes, but we are never wrong about what we like.

Jung's use of the word *feeling* to describe a rational, mental process has led to misunderstandings and confusion. This confusion is compounded in the English language by the fact that the word *feeling* has many meanings. It is used to describe emotions, such as "I'm feeling angry," and it also refers to tactile sensations, as in "That shirt feels rough on my skin." Jung was aware of this confusion, and he attempted to be very precise in defining what he meant by the feeling function. He specified that the feeling function was distinct from emotions (Jung 1921, par. 681). He stated that emotions and affect were synonymous terms and were "characterized by marked physical innervation on the one hand and a peculiar disturbance of the ideational process on the other" (ibid.). The feeling function, he asserted, was distinct from emotions and affect. He did state that when the feeling function was not conscious, it could include emotional components.

Note that Jung said emotions can affect the ideational process as well as the physiologic body. Emotions can spill over into any of the psychological functions — sensation, intuition, and thinking, as well as feeling. In fact, they do so when the functions are poorly developed and exist as inferior aspects of the personality.

Jung reiterated many times the distinction between the feeling function and emotions. For example, when he was giving the Tavistock lectures, he was asked to clarify the distinction between emotions and feeling. He replied: "There are definitely feelings which do not change the physiological condition. These feelings are very mental, they are not of an emotional nature" (Jung 1935, par. 58). Jung went on to state that differentiated feeling is a rational function of discriminating values: "It can be something as abstract as abstract thinking" (ibid.).

I want to draw your attention to the distinction Jung is making between emotions and mental processes in the statement quoted above: "These feelings are *mental*, they are not of an emotional nature." I want to stress this distinction because Jung excluded emotions from the differentiated, mental functions in this theory of psychological types. Jung saw the differentiated functions as mental processes. This is a fact which most users of his typology overlook. Emotions have to be considered in human behavior but they are not a part of the differentiated psychological types. I will return to the discussion of emotions shortly.

In the quote above, concerning the four functions (p. 30), Jung stated that "for complete orientation all four functions should contribute equally." This means that complete perceptions require that we use both sensation and intuition and that the best judgments require both thinking and feeling. Using sensation without intuition, we are locked into what exists in the here and now and are limited to viewing our world from one perspective. Using intuition without sensation, we are rarely in the present, speculating instead about the past and what could have been, or imagining future possibilities endlessly. We need both sensation and intuition in harmony if we are to perceive with our full human potential. Similarly, if we are to make the best decisions, we need to utilize both thinking and feeling. Thinking when used alone may be efficient, but without the balance of feeling, it is cold and inhumane. Feeling brings in the human factors of empathy and sympathy, but when used alone to make decisions may result in impractical, financially disastrous outcomes. It takes the positive aspects of both rational functions, of both thinking and feeling, to arrive at the best judgments.

When Jung divided the four functions into perceiving and judging pairs, he noted the general personality differences that would occur when a perceiving function, that is when either sensation or intuition, predominated in one's psychology as opposed to when a judging function, either thinking or feeling, predominated in one's psychological makeup. Jung stated that sensation and intuition have nothing to do with interpretations or evaluations. "They do not proceed selectively, according to principles [or values], they are simply receptive to what happens" (Jung 1921, par. 539). When either of the perceiving functions predominate in the psychological makeup of individuals, spontaneity, flexibility, and openness to change are evident in their personalities. These people accept life as it is and are able to "go with the flow," taking what life offers as it unfolds. When they are going to take a vacation, for example, they usually prefer to take off without calling ahead and reserving a motel room. For these perceiving individuals, structure, planning, and organization are experienced as unnecessary, limiting, and boring.

When the rational functions, either thinking or feeling, predominate in the psychological makeup, individuals experience a desire for structure and organization in their lives. They dislike leaving anything to chance. If they are taking a vacation, they want to know where they will be going, what they will be doing, and where they will be staying. They view planning as an efficient use of their energy. These individuals need to know what lies ahead and do not like surprises. They want to be prepared and, as a rule, do not like it when their plans are changed. With this rational, judging personality, individuals are predictable. For them, reliability and consistency are valuable attributes. Their friends and family know them as dependable people.

It is very common for judging personalities to view perceiving personalities as irresponsible space cadets, while the perceiving space-cadet personalities view them as boring and repetitious. It is possible to develop a personality in which both the perceiving and the judging tendencies are balanced. When this occurs, individuals are at ease with or without structure. There will be times when these people see the value of planning ahead and so that is what they do, effectively using their time and energy. There will be other times when they want to be free of all planning in order to be open and responsive. These individuals with a balance of judging and perceiving functions have enough flexibility to adapt to new situations with grace and ease and are not frustrated when their plans change.

Table I. Interaction of Perceiving–Judging with Introversion–Extraversion

	Perceiving – Flexible, adaptive to change	Balanced – Flexible and organized	Judging – Organized priorities, structured life
Introversion – Focus on the inner world	Flexible, inner focus	Flexible & organized, with inner focus	Organized & structured, with inner focus
Balanced – Both inner and physical worlds	Flexible, balancing inner & outer focus	Flexible & organized, balanced inner & outer focus	Organized & structured, balanced inner & outer focus
Extraversion – Focused on the physical world	Flexible, outer focus	Flexible & organized, with outer focus	Organized & structured, with outer focus

As we begin to examine our own personalities, the dimension of judging vs. perceiving is as important as the dimension of introversion vs. extraversion. With just these two dimensions from Jung's theory of psychological types, we begin to discover the varieties of human behavior. We can make a basic grid to picture the nine possible variations in personality functioning these two dimensions afford us.

A person could be balanced in regard to perceiving and judging and be highly extraverted, meaning that he or she was adaptable. Although such a person liked to make plans, a change in plans would not be upsetting. And being extraverted, such a person would focus primarily on the outer, physical world. Or a person could be balanced in regard to introversion and extraversion and be high on the judging dimension. This person would spend approximately equal time focusing on the inner subjective world and the outer physical world. But such a person would want order and structure in both worlds. The seven other combinations resulting from the interaction of judging–perceiving with introversion–extraversion produce personality styles that are distinctive.

What has been discussed thus far is classic Jung. The three-by-three table is only a different perspective for viewing the concepts that Jung described, and these nine categories do not exhaust the possibilities for typological functioning. It is also true that an individual may be described by one category at one time and another category at another time. The finer distinctions of the categories arise when we examine which of the judging functions or which of the perceiving functions is most frequently used by the individual.

When Jung wrote about psychological types, he emphasized the interaction of the individual functions with the orientations of introversion and extraversion. He described eight different combinations of function and orientation: introverted sensation, extraverted sensation, introverted intuition, extraverted intuition, introverted thinking, extraverted thinking, introverted feeling, and extraverted feeling. These eight modes provide the basic structure of Jung's theory. It is these eight modes which clarify the global concepts of introversion, extraversion, judging, and perceiving, telling us in which ways we are introverted, for example, or just how we are organized, judging personalities.

These eight modes, the combinations of the four functions with the two orientations, comprise the totality of the methods we use to receive and process information. Our interactions with both our inner and outer worlds are dependent upon them. They are the ways through which we know ourselves and our environments. Since Jung specified that the eight modes are mental functions which, in their true essence, are separate from emotions, they may be viewed as cognitive modes. The word *cognitive* derives from *cognoscere*, which means "to know." These eight modes are our ways of knowing and will be referred to as cognitive modes in this work. All eight cognitive modes are operating to a greater or lesser extent in each personality. The relative development of eight cognitive modes within an individual's personality comprises that person's cognitive style. (A description of the eight cognitive modes can be found in Chapter 7. A discussion of how these cognitive modes may be assessed follows in the next chapter.)

Jung's use of the cross image as a heuristic device to explain the four functions is not applicable to describing how the eight cognitive modes interact. The cross image is too restrictive. It was a simplistic device to depict the four functions but it is a Procrustean fit for the eight cognitive modes.

The image of the cross reinforced the idea of oppositions and of preferring or developing one function at the expense of another function. But permanent oppositions, as we have noted, are contrary to Jung's basic premise that the resolution of opposites is the aim and goal of an individual moving toward increased consciousness. It becomes obvious, as we examine Jung's theory of psychological types more closely, that Jung utilized the symbol of the cross as a teaching device to explain how he conceived the four functions to be interacting in an unaware, unconscious individual personality.

The cross itself is an incomplete image. The way it was used by Jung forces a static interpretation of typology and does not provide a picture of how the individuation process proceeds. But let's look at the image of the cross more closely and compare it to the image of the medicine wheel discussed in Chapter 1. The medicine wheel offers an image of wholeness with the symbol of the circle, encompassing a cross. The cross alone is incomplete because it lacks the circle. Jung was aware that the image of a cross within a circle was a universal symbol of wholeness but he did not use it when he first explained his theory. The cross may be representative of where Jung, the scientist, was in the development of his theory of psychological types.

The medicine wheel, as I see it, is a more appropriate symbol of psychological typology than the cross. The medicine wheel encompasses the total personality and can be expanded to include the emotional, physical, mental, spiritual, and sexual aspects of a human being. The separation between the emotional and mental functioning is clear when we use the medicine wheel. Human emotions do affect mental functioning but they are a distinctly separate process. Emotions affect mental processes, that is, they affect the four typological functions when the functions are not differentiated. Jung stated that rudimentary, undeveloped functions would break into a person's behavior laden with emotion. The picture of how these emotions and mental functions interact is not given with the image of the cross and the separation of mental and emotional processes is fuzzy in his theory. When human emotions affect mental processes, it is a contamination.

On the medicine wheel, the mental aspects are in the north of the wheel, opposite the emotional aspects in the south. If we return to the medicine wheel and use that as our vantage point,

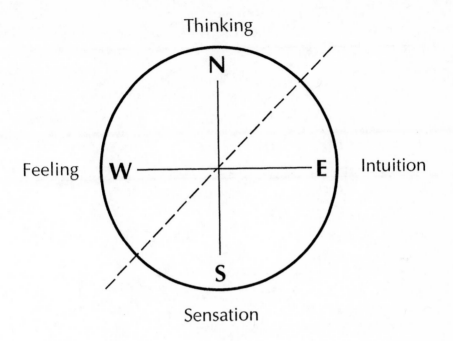

Figure 6. *Arrangement of the Four Functions within the Wind Mind Wheel*

we can reconceptualize how typology fits into the human personality.

In the north of the medicine wheel is the mind wheel. The mind wheel is a developmental wheel depicting a progression from water mind, which has no standpoint, to wind mind. Wind mind is the mind which tries to comprehend through dualities. As it reaches for understanding, the wind mind categorizes by taking things apart and arranging them in oppositions. The four typological functions, which Jung repeatedly stated were mental functions, belong in the wind mind, the place of oppositions. But the arrangement of the four functions within the wind mind is not the arrangement Jung hypothesized. There is an opposition, but it is not between thinking and feeling or between sensation and intuition.

The arrangement of the four functions, as I envision them, is in accord with the Power of the Four Directions. In this arrangement, sensation is in the south, thinking in the north, feeling in the west, and intuition in the east.

The reason for placing sensation in the south is that the

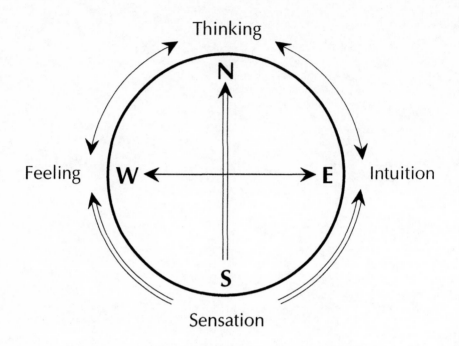

Figure 7. Possible Interactions Between the Four Functions

south is the starting place in teaching wheels and the place of trust and innocence. Sensation is the first of the functions. It records what is, without bias, unselectively, and it is the only function that can work by itself. Thinking is placed in the north because the power of the north has to do with wisdom and logic. Logic is the thinking function. The feeling function is placed in the west. The power of the west connects to the earth and the physical body. It is the place of bodily knowing. Often our values of what we like and dislike are difficult to articulate but we still know what we like. The feeling function and our values are part of our bodily knowing. The east is the place of fire and the sparks of illumination. It is the place of unlimited imagination. Intuition belongs here.

There is an opposition in this typology mind wheel. It is an opposition between the judging functions and the perceiving functions. Thinking and feeling together are opposed to sensation and intuition. This, I think, is the basic opposition in the typological functioning. This opposition reflects the basic difference between organized, judging individuals and spontaneously reactive, perceptive individuals.

On this typology wheel, all combinations of mental functioning are possible. Sensation can combine with intuition, if the individual's mental energy flows to the right on the wheel. It can combine with feeling if the energy moves to the left, or with thinking if the energy bridges across the circle. Sensation must be present in any mental functioning. That is a given and this medicine wheel model depicts that fact since the energy must begin in the south. The variations in the combinations possible with the image of the medicine wheel are more complex than those allowed by the cross image. For example, the energy originating in sensation could move to feeling and the two could combine with thinking. With this model, mental faculties need not be limited to an interaction between one perceiving and one judging function, as Jung originally hypothesized.

I have not placed introversion and extraversion on the mind wheel because they are not mental functions. Introversion and extraversion are orientations describing whether the individual is focused on the inner, subjective world or the outer, physical world. Introversion and extraversion could be placed on the initial, basic medicine wheel as there is a compatibility between them and two aspects of the Powers of the Four Directions. Introversion would be in the west, the place of introspection and insight, the place of going within the physical body to find the light within the dark. Extraversion would be in the east, the place of the illuminating sun, the place of enlightenment gained from observing the physical world.

Using the framework of the medicine wheel frees typology from the artificial constraints imposed by the inherent oppositions of the cross symbol. Also, the basic medicine wheel cleanly separates the mental and emotional aspects of the human personality. Emotions can contaminate mental functioning when the mental functions are not developed. Emotions are an essential part of human functioning but they are separate from mental functioning.

As we shall see in the next chapter, the medicine wheel image is also compatible with the results of empirical research into the dynamics of Jung's theory. We shall see how the medicine wheel, this ancient, archetypal image, is still relevant today. There is much that we can become aware of by ourselves, as we move toward increased consciousness, but often we want another opinion, another mirror to reflect our functioning to us. One possible mirror and how it evolved will be discussed next. It is the story of the development of the *Singer-Loomis Inventory of Personality.*

Chapter 4

The Development of the
Singer-Loomis Inventory of
Personality

In the Spirit of Jung, the Scientist

In 1977, my colleague June Singer and I began to investigate the dynamics of Jung's theory of psychological types. We were aware that Jung's creative work was distinguished by his willingness to change and refine his theories as new data accumulated. It was in accord with that spirit of Jung, the scientist, that June Singer and I embarked on our investigation which eventually led us to develop a new personality inventory, the Singer-Loomis Inventory of Personality (SLIP). When we began our research, we had no quarrel with Jung's conceptual definitions of the four functions or his descriptions of the orientations of introversion and extraversion, but we did question whether the dynamics of his theory were valid.

The pictorial representation of the cross, which Jung offered to depict the interrelationship of the four functions, buttressed the idea that the dynamics of typology depended upon opposition and led many people to view typology as a static system that could classify people into permanent, discrete categories. This is contrary to Jung's intentions, as noted in the previous chapter in the quote from the Tavistock lectures where he refused to type anyone (1935, par. 34). Locking people into fixed categories according to oppositions is also contrary to the Jungian process of individuation, which is based upon the eventual union or transcendence of opposites.

June Singer and I, puzzled by the contradiction between the static dynamic of typology, as it was taught and understood by Jungians and non-Jungians alike, and the living dynamic of the individuation process, began to question the bipolarity assumption in Jung's theory of psychological types. We knew that the hallmark of creative individuals was flexibility in their mental processes. This core characteristic of being able to do the unexpected, to view life from two perspectives at once, Janus-like, was documented in research on creative individuals and discussed in theoretical hypotheses which developed from creativity research (Dellas and Gaier 1970, Helson 1971, Rothenberg 1971). Was it necessarily true, we wondered, that feeling is always the inferior function when thinking is the most highly developed? What about all the creative individuals who didn't seem to be conforming to the bipolarity dynamic?

In addition to our theoretical musings, June and I also shared the experience of feeling that we had been falsely typed, that is, our knowledge of ourselves did not conform to the profiles we had obtained from personality tests measuring typology. We knew of several other individuals who were likewise disconcerted by their profiles. These individuals had complained, as we ourselves had, that there were many items on the typology inventories where they experienced difficulty choosing their answer, because they wanted either to select or reject both options.

As we examined the two prominent inventories measuring typology, the Grey-Wheelwrights Jungian Type Survey (GW) and the Myers-Briggs Type Indicator (MBTI), it became apparent why the personality profiles obtained by these two instruments always fulfilled Jung's oppositional dynamic. Both the GW and the MBTI continually supported Jung's ideas of superior, inferior, and auxiliary functions because of the format of the items comprising those inventories. All of the items in both inventories were forced choice, and the forced choice was always between the oppositional pair Jung depicted in his cross image. This means the person taking the inventory could choose between a thinking or a feeling response, for example, or between a sensation or an intuitive response. There were no other options; when the subject selects one alternative, the other is rejected. The circularity generated by the format of the GW and the MBTI which supported Jung's bipolarity hypothesis bothered us. It also became clear why neither of these instruments could reveal the typology of a creative individual. Forced choice items would not allow it.

June and I decided to test empirically Jung's bipolar assumption using the GW and the MBTI in our study. We reasoned that if Jung's bipolarity assumption was correct, that is, if the oppositional arrangement of the functions was inherent within the individual psyche, then it was not necessary to use forced-choice questions to assess an individual's typology. On the other hand, if Jung's bipolarity assumption was not valid, changing the forced-choice items in the GW and the MBTI to another format would have an effect on the resulting profiles.

In our study, each forced-choice item in the GW and the MBTI was replaced by two scaled-response items. For example, the GW item:

> At a party I like to:
> a. talk
> b. listen

was replaced by two items separated in the test:

> At a party I like to talk.
> At a party I like to listen.

The subject would respond to the scaled items by indicating never, sometimes, half the time, usually, or always. Further, if a single forced-choice item was doubly weighted, it was replaced with four scaled-response items.

The subjects in our study were given the original version of either the GW or the MBTI and our revised version of the same test. If Jung's bipolarity assumption is correct, then a person taking the original test and a rewritten version of that test would have the same superior, inferior, and auxiliary functions in both profiles. The results from this study are shown in the table below.

Sixty-one percent of the individuals who participated in this research did not have the same superior function on the

Table II. Results of SLIP Research

	GW	MBTI	TOTAL
Number of subjects in the study	120	79	199
Changes in superior function	86 (72%)	36 (46%)	122 (61%)
Inferior not opposed to superior	66 (55%)	29 (36%)	95 (48%)

revised, rewritten version as they had had on the original version. Further, on the revised version, almost half of them (48 percent) did not have an inferior function that was the hypothesized opposite of their superior function.

We were surprised by the magnitude of our results. The fact that three out of five people showed a different superior function when only the format of the items was revised led us to wonder whether the functions were being accurately assessed by the inventories we used in our research. To us, the need for a new test to measure typology was apparent. (For a full discussion of this research, see Loomis and Singer 1980.)

We were determined to develop an instrument to measure typology that would be theoretically and empirically sound. We would be true to Jung's concepts, and we would adhere to the guidelines of test construction published by the American Psychological Association. At each step in the development of the SLIP, we have been mindful of our original intent.

I cannot emphasize too strongly that there was never a conceptual disagreement with Jung's theory. We concurred with his descriptions of the four functions and with his concepts of the rational and irrational pairs. We also acknowledged the validity of the introverted and extraverted orientations. Our quandary centered only on the dynamics of his theory. We saw typology as a dynamic process and agreed with those, including Jung himself, who would use typology as a roadmap for the individuation process.

June and I decided that a more accurate assessment of psychological functioning, and one truer to Jung's intentions, could be obtained if the eight cognitive modes, namely, introverted sensation, extraverted sensation, introverted intuition, extraverted intuition, introverted thinking, extraverted thinking, introverted feeling, and extraverted feeling, were measured independently by scaled-response items. The scores obtained for these eight scales could then be combined to yield scores for introversion, extraversion, judging, perceiving, thinking, feeling, sensation, and intuition. Each stage of the SLIP's development was rigorously examined by experimental design and statistical analyses. (A fuller explanation of these steps may be found in the SLIP Manual, Singer and Loomis 1984, and Loomis and Singer 1987.) Our descriptions of the eight cognitive modes were drawn from Jung's conceptualizations of the differentiated functions. This meant that any reference to an implied inferiority was excluded. For example, in describing introverted thinking or extraverted thinking, we omitted any reference to inferior feeling judgments.

The SLIP has been through two major revisions; the current edition is the third edition of the inventory. The final revision, which will remove the experimental label from the SLIP, will not be a major overhaul, but rather a fine tuning of the instrument. With what I am proposing in this book, there will also be a new way to view the results, a way that incorporates the Native American medicine wheel. Up until now, SLIP results have been presented in a bar graph form or, as I suggested in Chapter 3, in a three-by-three table. The best way to view one's typology, I believe, is to use the medicine wheel of the functions and incorporate introversion and extraversion into that wheel. With the cognitive modes depicted as eight points on the medicine wheel, the wheel would look like this:

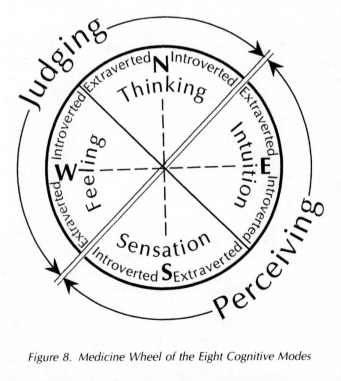

Figure 8. Medicine Wheel of the Eight Cognitive Modes

Standing on the perimeter of the medicine wheel, the introverted orientation of the function is on the left and the extraverted orientation of the function is on the right. This conforms to the Native American idea that the left side is the receiving side and the right side is the giving or outward-moving side. The center is the void, the origin, or matrix of the functions. Plotting percentages, provided by the SLIP profile, for each of the eight cognitive modes from the center outward would give a pictorial representation of one's cognitive style. Whether one is more judging or perceiving, more introverted or extraverted, is readily visible. Further, and more importantly, the way in which one is introverted or is perceiving is graphically depicted by the development of the individual cognitive modes.

At this time, norms for specific populations are being compiled by Edwin Olson. This enables an individual profile to be compared to others in a similar field, for example, someone working in organizational development could compare her profile with the norms for others in that field of endeavor. (In fact, this is the area of Olson's specific interest. He is also developing other materials to use with the SLIP in organizational settings.)

The SLIP provides an objective mirror to view how one is functioning typologically. By measuring the eight cognitive modes independently and not artificially imposing bipolarity on the resulting profiles, the SLIP is able to depict creative personalities when they exist. These personalities, for example, may be those where introverted thinking and extraverted feeling are both differentiated and highly developed. If, however, a bipolar development of the cognitive modes characterizes the individual's personality, the SLIP will reveal that.

It is possible to gain some insights into one's typological functioning by self-assessment. That is the purpose of this book. Self-assessment, however, because of our own bias and inability to see our own shadow, may not provide as clear a mirror as the SLIP provides, but it is a step toward increased consciousness. In the following chapters, we will look at how Jung used typology as a roadmap for the individuation process and how typology can be combined with Native American teachings to form the basis for one's growth toward increased consciousness.

Chapter 5

Jung's Theory of Typology and the Individuation Process

Jung's theory of psychological types is a roadmap for the individuation process. It is that simple. That was Jung's intent as he developed his theory, yet few people have comprehended this fact (Meier 1971). The four functions — thinking, feeling, intuition, and sensation — are the compass points on our inner mindscape, enabling us to locate where we are standing on our path toward increased consciousness. We determine where we are by recognizing which cognitive modes we use the most frequently and which cogitive modes we feel uneasy about. Jung said, "Consciousness rests on the four elements or basic functions" (1935, par. 261), and developing the full potential of human consciousness requires having all four functions differentiated and working in harmony (1921, par. 518). If developing our full potential is the goal we are seeking, then typology can outline the process by showing us where we are and where we have yet to travel to reach our destination. The roadmap is clear but many people cannot read it because utilizing this map demands self-awareness, consciousness.

There is a pervasive idea of the journey toward wholeness being an automatic process that unfolds naturally in the course of a lifetime. Jung contributed to the popularity of this idea when he wrote:

> The transcendent function does not proceed without aim and purpose, but leads to the revelation of the essential man. It is in the first place a purely natural process, which may in some cases pursue its course without the knowledge or assistance of the individual, and can sometimes forcibly accomplish itself in the face of opposition. The meaning and purpose of the process is the

realization, in all its aspects, of the personality originally hidden away in the embryonic germ-plasm; the production and unfurling of the original, potential wholeness. . . . For these reasons I have termed this the individuation process. (1943, par. 186)

From this quote, it would appear that we do not have to take responsibility for the process of individuation, that if we live long enough, the unlived side will be lived. But there is a catch here. In this purely "natural process," wholeness is not consciously attained. This is an important distinction.

Jung called upon the psychological process of enantiodromia to explain how this "natural process" could lead to individuals living out all of their human potential. *Enantio* means opposites, *dromia* means course or process. *Enantiodromia* refers to one thing becoming its opposite across time. An extraverted man, for example, if he lives long enough, will experience his introverted nature. However, as Jung noted, when enantiodromia is the process involved in living the unlived side, this switch to the opposite personality trait or traits is often without the conscious awareness of the individual.

The elder statesman who retires from politics and national affairs to pursue painting and gardening is an example of enantiodromia at work. The mid-life crises experienced by multitudes of individuals can also be viewed as an attempt of their Higher Self to force them to give expression to the unlived, neglected side of their personalities. The unlived side may be lived, but when consciousness is absent, the previously lived side disappears. Enantiodromia, by definition, cannot lead to conscious wholeness. One thing is replaced by another. In regard to typology, the comment is often made that a function or orientation is worn out in middle or later years by overuse and is replaced with another function or the opposite orientation. The archetypal pattern for this "natural process" of enantiodromia is told in the fairy tale, "Three Feathers."

An old king, aware of his advancing years and approaching infirmity, began to wonder which of his three sons should inherit his kingdom after his death.

Two of his sons were strong. The third, and youngest son, was a weakling. He was called Dumling or Blockhead. As the king wrestled with his problem, he decided to hold a contest for his sons with the winner to be declared the future king. He called his sons together, explaining that each of them was to blow a feather in the air and then to follow the direction of the feather and find a carpet. The one who returned with the finest carpet would be the winner.

The three sons did as they were bidden. The first strong son blew his feather, and it went to the right. The second strong son blew his feather, and it floated to the left. Dumling blew his feather, and it fell straight to the ground. The strong sons, jeering at their brother, embarked on their quest. Dumling, not knowing what else to do, remained where he was. Looking down on his feather, Dumling noticed a trap door. He lifted it and discovered a flight of stairs descending into the earth. Following the stairs down, Dumling arrived at the court of a toad queen. When the toad queen asked why he had come, Dumling explained his plight. The toad queen gave Dumling a beautiful carpet, finer than any on earth. Dumling returned to his father. His brothers also returned. But they, never expecting any competition from Dumling, had settled for homespun shepherd's cloth. The king declared Dumling the winner, but his two brothers objected strenuously, saying that Dumling was such a simpleton, he would not be able to rule the kingdom wisely. The king yielded to their arguments and set another task for his sons.

This time the king told his sons: "Whoever returns with the most beautiful ring will inherit the kingdom." Again the feathers were blown. One son went to the right, another to the left, and Dumling again followed his feather to the earth and the realm of the toad queen. This time Dumling was given a jeweled gold and silver ring, and he returned to his father. His brothers returned with metal rings from the harness of a carriage horse. But again they pleaded with the king for another contest. They could not yield to Dumling.

The third contest was for a bride. And again, clearly, Dumling was the winner. He brought home a beautiful princess, who underground had been one of the small toads attending the toad queen. His brothers returned with peasant women who happened to be the first women they encountered. The king declared Dumling the winner, stating: "The kingdom must now belong to my youngest son after my death."

The two older sons begged for just one more contest, this one to determine the strength of the women they had chosen as their brides. Again the king consented to their request. The contest, jumping through a hoop, was won easily by the princess. The other two women injured themselves. One broke an arm, the other a leg. The youngest son married the princess, and after his father's death, we're told, he ruled the kingdom for many years with wisdom and justice.

Viewing this fairy tale as depicting the "natural process" of the four typological functions operating in an individual's personality, or, more accurately, as the interaction of the four functions within a man's personality, the king would symbolize the highly developed, dominant function. The fairy tale does not specify which function the king represents. It could be any of the four. The two strong sons are auxiliary functions, cooperating with the dominant function but subordinate to it. Dumling, the third son, is the undeveloped fourth function. The inferior function connects to the inner world. We know this is the tale of a man's development because, in this tale, the connection is to the neglected, feminine side of the personality. The toad queen resides deep within the earth, the realm of the feminine. Tales of a woman connecting with her masculine side always involve a frog—a prince or handsome youth transformed into a frog, never a toad. That the feminine must be united with the masculine in the story "Three Feathers" is also symbolized by the ring, a gold and silver ring, which the toad queen gives to Dumling.

Dumling cannot become king, the story tells us, until the old king dies. The inferior function cannot be developed until the dominant function yields. There is always one dominant in this hierarchical model; nowhere do the four functions unite. There is always a king, but there is never consciousness. There is a new dominant function, but the old dominant function disappears. The wholeness that the four functions working in unison would provide is absent. This is the process of enantiodromia. It is a process different from the process of conscious individuation via the transcendent function.

Jung used the metaphor of alchemy to explain how individuation proceeds by means of the transcendent function. He said: "The secret of alchemy was in fact the transcendent function, the transformation of the personality through the blending and fusion of the noble with the base components, of the differentiated with the inferior functions, of the conscious with the unconscious" (1928, par. 360). When individuation is conscious, the old dominant function does not disappear. It blends and fuses with the new.

When Jung used the term *transcendent function* in his state-ment regarding the "natural process" of individuation, he mis-spoke. He was actually referring to the Self, the higher power within each of us that pushes us to experience all that it means to be human. Our higher Self works independently of our con-sciousness. The transcendent function, on the other hand, entails the conscious will and intent of the individual. Where you begin the process of individuation depends on what your unconscious, your inner Self, mirrors as a problem of one-sidedness for you. Until your one-sidedness is resolved by your determination to engage the opposite aspect of your personality and give birth to the transcendent function, a process that can feel like a crucifixion, you cannot state that you have a prefer-ence for one psychological function over another. Preference implies choice, and until two or more of the functions are incorporated and equally developed, you are not choosing, selecting, or preferring one function over the other. Without equal access to the functions, a person is not exhibiting a pref-erence for one function over another, but rather a habitual, automatic pattern of interactions. The transcendent function, earned by hard work, provides a bridge between two aspects of the personality previously separated. According to Jung, a bridge is often the symbol of the transcendent function in dreams. With a bridge, both sides are equally accessible to the individual. Typologically, this means that two functions, pre-viously considered opposites, would be equally well developed, or that the individual would be both introverted and extraverted.

The habitual way we operate represents the way we have adapted to society. It is an integral part of our persona. In regard to typology and persona, Jung has this to say:

> The persona is always identical with a typical attitude domi-nated by a single psychological function, for example by think-ing, feeling, or intuition. This one-sidedness necessarily results in the relative repression of the other functions. In consequence the persona is an obstacle to the individual's development. The dissolution of the persona is therefore an indispensable condi-tion for individuation. (1928, par. 487)

In order to dissolve the persona, we must know what func-tion and which orientation we have relied upon in our adaptation to society. We cannot remove the mask we wear until we know what the mask is. As mentioned earlier, the dissolution of the persona does not mean the destruction of the persona, but a dissolution of the ego's identification with the persona. We will always have social roles to fill, but we want to be conscious of what role we are playing. The dissolution of an overidentification with one's persona comes about through an expansion of one's ego ideal.

Everything that is excluded from one's ego ideal falls into the shadow. What does this mean typologically? Jung writes:

> By shadow I mean the "negative" side of the personality, the sum of all those unpleasant qualities we like to hide, together with the insufficiently developed functions and the contents of the personal unconscious. (1943, par. 103)

Thus, in regard to persona and shadow, the utilized, developed psychological function is identified with the persona, and the neglected or inferior functions are relegated to the shadow. For example, if I have said to myself that I will not be critical of others, I am relegating to my shadow my critical judging faculties. Typologically, I am limiting my extraverted thinking and extraverted sensation. I may also be denying my introverted feeling.

As you integrate the unlived side through the development of the transcendent function, you do not lose what you have already developed, you augment your abilities, your consciousness. But it is not always easy to determine which functions and cognitive modes we are using because the eight cognitive modes interact in complex ways. Even determining whether introversion or extraversion is the orientation of the moment is often difficult. Yet introversion and extraversion are one pair of opposites that must be reconciled. Jung writes that the two orientations of introversion and extraversion "ought in their harmonious alternation, to give life a rhythm, but it seems to require a high degree of art to achieve such a rhythm" (1943, par. 87). And for the process of individuation, "the union of opposites is necessary and in particular the difficult task of reconciling extraversion and introversion by means of the transcendent function" (Jung 1954, par. 803).

Introversion implies a solitary process, but extraversion also can be a solitary pursuit. If I am alone, for example, envisioning how to arrange the furniture in my home, or imagining what a new building will look like, or reflecting on how the events of the previous day could have been improved, I am engaged in a solitary process. But because my focus, that is the problem I am considering, concerns outer reality, my orientation, although I am alone, is extraverted. It is a mistake to assume that extraversion always entails working or being with other people.

It is true that working with others often is an extraverted orientation. For example, if there is a collaborative effort focused on external reality, say, a husband and a wife deciding where they want to vacation or a committee investigating ways to protect schoolchildren from the impact of drugs, then there definitely is an extraverted orientation shared with others. But what of a committee focusing on civil rights issues? Although the committee's interrelationships are extraverted and the impact of civil rights affects external behavior, the primary focus of the committee is on an idea, an abstract value, an inner reality. The primary focus is introverted. Nothing is simple when we move into analyzing the mind.

Reconciling the opposites of introversion and extraversion is difficult, and that may be where one has to start. But a person is not introverted in every function, nor always extraverted. The eight cognitive modes are constantly interacting with each other. Similarly, it may be equally difficult for those individuals whose task will be the reconciliation of a rational, judging, structured life with an irrational, perceiving adaptability, for no one is always structured, organized, or planning ahead.

Where do we begin? If the transcendent function "arises from the union of conscious and unconscious contents" (Jung 1958, par. 131), just exactly what are we talking about? What is the something that is conscious? And what is its unconscious opposite? Our emotions often help guide the process, indicating to us where our one-sidedness exists. That which irritates us in others is often what we have rejected in ourselves. Our irritation or anger points out what we have relegated to our shadow. On the other hand, our comfort with certain people or admiration for others can help us identify what we have chosen to include in our persona, or chosen to value. The task is to identify the cognitive modes embodied in our projections.

A Native American teaching called the Star Maiden Circle

offers a different perspective for examining our persona and shadow and our typology. It provides an opportunity to examine where we have been caught in a repeating pattern of habitual behaviors. It can also provide some insights as to why we are the way we are. Until we can see where we are caught, where we have relied on certain cognitive modes and ignored others, we cannot begin to free ourselves to move forward on our path toward increased consciousness. The teachings of the Star Maiden Circle also allow us to examine where our emotions and projections can become guides for this process.

The use of a medicine wheel to depict our personality is in accord with Jung's ideas. He wrote: "One's given personality could be represented by a continuous circle, whereas the conscious personality would be a circle divided up in a definite way" (1935, par. 261). The Star Maiden Circle and what it has to offer are examined in the next chapter.

Chapter 6

The Star Maiden Circle

The Star Maiden Circle is a key teaching wheel, illustrating the psychological aspects of human life. With the picture, the overview, that the Star Maiden Circle provides, we are given an Archimedean point outside of ourselves from which we can examine our lives in detail. The Star Maiden Circle is an ancient teaching, reinterpreted in the language of today. It is as applicable to our lives today as it was applicable to those who lived hundreds of years ago. Our outer world may have changed since those ancient times, but our inner world and the dynamics of our inner lives remain remarkably similar to those of our ancestors.

The Star Maiden Circle, as with all medicine wheels, incorporates the Powers of the Four Directions. Briefly, this means that, although not explicitly stated, the south of the wheel is the place of trust and innocence; it is the place of giving and of flowing human emotions. The west is the place of holding with the physical body, the place of introspection and insight. The north is the place of receiving with the mind and the location of wisdom and logic. The east is the place of determining with the spirit; it is the place of illumination and enlightenment.

The process of life depicted by the Star Maiden Circle begins in the south and cycles clockwise. The eight points on the circle represent the psychological realities operating in our lives. As we step onto the circle in the south, we begin this life movement in the area of mythologies; there is always a myth, an archetypal pattern, underlying our life, and it influences all that we do whether we are conscious of the myth or not. The myth we are living is incorporated in our persona. It may be that the myth is Great Mother, Warrior, Teacher, or Priest.

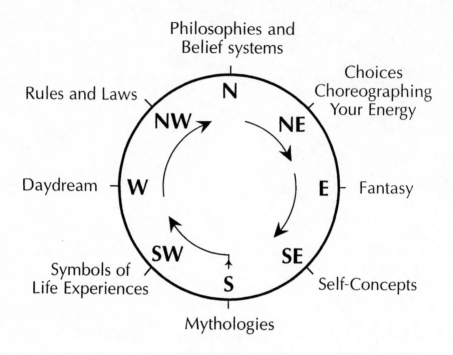

Figure 9. The Star Maiden Circle

Whatever the myth, life is experienced from that particular perspective. On the Star Maiden Circle, this is shown as a movement from the south to the southwest, the place indicated as the symbols of life experiences. The particular experiences of life that we have are interpreted from the perspective of the myth we are living, creating symbols for us of what life is about. We then move to the west, the area of the daydream.

In these teachings, the life we are living in this physical reality, this third dimension, is called the dream. So the daydream, the dream of the day, refers to how we are living our lives, how we are actualizing and becoming the persons we believe we are. According to the Star Maiden Circle, life is actualized in accordance with the myth we hold about ourselves. This means that our persona is the ultimate determiner of who we will become. From the west, the movement of life proceeds to the northwest and enters the area of rules and laws. It is here that we decide what we should and should not do and what is right and what is wrong. Often the rules and laws that we establish for ourselves are based on what we have been taught by family, society, and religion, but always these rules and laws are aligned with the myths we hold about ourselves.

As we live life, the area of rules and laws extends into the realm of philosophies and belief systems, shown on the north of the Star Maiden Circle. The philosophies and belief systems that we embrace are used not only to govern our lives but to determine for others how they should be living their lives. Now it is not only what we should do but what everyone should do to live a moral and just life. The movement of life depicted on the Star Maiden Circle next enters the northeast, the place of choices. It is here, with our choices, that we decide what changes we can make in our lives. Our choices, as illustrated on the Star Maiden Circle, are based on our philosophies and beliefs, our rules and laws, what we are actualizing, what we have experienced, and at the root of it all, on the mythologies we hold.

As the cycle of life continues, it moves to the place of fantasy in the east. It is here that we envision what is possible for ourselves in this lifetime. Again, what we imagine for ourselves is colored by our mythology, by our persona, and all that has preceded on the Star Maiden Circle. From the place of fantasy and imagination, the cycle of life moves to the southeast; how we image ourselves feeds directly into our self-concepts. The cycle of life repeats as our concepts of self are aligned with the myths we are living out. Or, as Jungians would say, our concepts of self are aligned with the myths that are living us.

There are two major movements for the Star Maiden Circle. One is the dark dance, the other the light dance. The dark dance, the dance of all those individuals who have not begun the process of individuation, is called the Circle of Foxes. Everyone begins life on the Circle of Foxes. It is the dance we begin as children, and it is a movement of a repeating pattern of behavior where we have no awareness of the pattern. When we are on the Circle of Foxes, we are like the fox enamored with the beauty of its own tail, circling repetitively, attempting to catch the beauty, but succeeding only in going around and around getting nowhere. We do not recognize that it is our own tail that eludes our grasp. Yet we are convinced that we are on the right path.

The Dark Dance

We enter the Circle of Foxes as wounded, needy, little children, and we usually stay on it into adulthood until some crisis—a painful life experience, an emotional or a physical illness—forces us to examine our life patterns and presents us with the opportunity for change. The Circle of Foxes provides a tool for us to use as we examine our lives, and it points out areas where changes are possible if we wish to make them.

We step onto the Circle of Foxes in the south, holding those particular core beliefs which, as children, we found gave meaning and direction to our lives. These particular beliefs were framed by a childish viewpoint and they are part of our persona, the mythology we hold about who we are. A core belief may be something, for example, like "Nothing in life is easy." "I will always have to work hard for what I want." "I won't say what I want because I'll never get it." Core beliefs and our central mythology were adaptive in childhood. They formed part of our ego defenses. As children, our myth may have been something like "The Tough Little Kid," "The Girl Who Endures," or "Daddy's Little Darling." As we grew, our myths

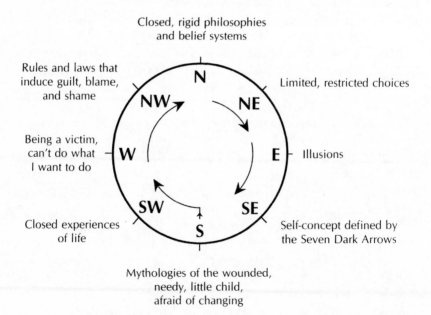

Figure 10. The Circle of Foxes Movement of the Star Maiden Circle

grew with us, and in becoming our persona, they may, for example, now embody the archetype of "Warrior," "Martyr," or "Helpless Maiden." Our myths and our core beliefs determine how we will live our lives and interact with the people around us. When we are on the Circle of Foxes, we identify ourselves completely with our myths, our persona, and these myths always include a pain tape.

Pain tapes are part of the price we pay to maintain our persona. They connect to those parts of ourselves that we have excluded, those parts of ourselves we have suppressed or denied in order to adapt to the world around us. For example, the little boy who sees himself as the "Tough Little Kid," who will not cry when he is hurt, who thinks he must do everything by himself, the hard way, has had to exclude tenderness, gentleness, and helplessness from his personality. He might grow into a man embodying the "Self-Reliant Warrior," unable to ask. for help, even when help is available. The overemphasis on independence in such a man can become a pain tape, preventing him from seeing how cooperation and interdependence can result in achieving successful solutions to problems with greater ease and more pleasure.

Locked into our myths, the movement depicted on the Circle of Foxes takes us into the experiencing of life in the southwest. What we are experiencing, however, is not all that life has to offer. We are open only to those experiences which validate our view of life and closed to those experiences which are incongruent with our mythology and core beliefs. Our mythology, with its core beliefs, becomes a self-fulfilling prophecy about how we will experience and symbolize life. The Self-Reliant Warrior, for example, may at sometime venture to ask another person to help him in what he sees as a worthwhile undertaking. If the other person is unwilling or unable to participate, the Warrior is reinforced in his belief that he must do things himself. And conversely, if by chance someone does cooperate with him, the Warrior views it as a fluke. It is seen as a chance happening and is quickly minimized or forgotten.

Moving into the west on the Circle of Foxes with our closed symbols of life experiences, we do not actualize our full potential. We actualize only that part of ourselves which is embodied in our persona, in our myth. We become the person our childish mind has framed. The Warrior, for example, may see all of life as a potential battle. He may, through discipline and hard work, develop his intellect and hone his competitiveness, achieving success in his chosen field. As a Warrior, however, in developing his intellect and maintaining his self-reliance, he probably has continued to exclude his gentle side. He may have severed his connection to his emotions and even convinced himself that he does not need relationships.

The life that is actualized on the Circle of Foxes is very limited. In this dark dance, we are often acutely aware of what has happened in the past and vigilant, if not worried, about what can happen in the future. As adults, we are fulfilling the image we have of ourselves but we are not aware of how limited that image is. Any pain this image may cost us is a pain familiar to us, and, in the dark dance, we prefer the known to the unknown. The unknown, from our perspective, could be even more painful.

The rules and laws governing behavior on the Circle of Foxes are interwoven with guilt and shame, and they reinforce the image we have of ourselves. From the perspective of the myth that is being lived and the core beliefs aligned with that myth, there is only one way for the individual to behave. There is an "either-or" mentality. Behavior is either right or it is wrong. This results in the individual feeling either proud and affirmed on the one hand, or ashamed and guilty on the other. Self-judging is based on the role being played, the myth being lived. The warrior, for example, would judge himself harshly, feeling guilty or ashamed, if he were not prepared for the task at hand, or if he saw himself as being weak and incompetent.

With the cycling of the life movement from the northwest to the north of the Circle of Foxes, all actions, one's own and those of other people, are viewed as good or bad, moral or immoral. One's personal rules of conduct are extended into a philosophy and belief system; and, where previously the rules and laws governed only one's own life, now as philosophies and belief systems, they are generalized to govern the lives of everyone.

It is possible for an individual to hold a unique viewpoint in regard to a philosophy or belief system, but, most frequently, the individual joins with others and together they share common values. Group members then induce guilt, blame, and shame in each other for any deviation from what their philosophy and belief system holds to be moral, proper behavior. The individual, contained within the group, is convinced that this philosophy and belief system is the right one and feels pity or scorn for anyone who does not share these values. The Warrior, for example, may join a group—a religious or political organization—whose philosophies and belief systems are congruent with his. The group buttresses his core beliefs, sharing his values of being prepared, being tough, being self-reliant. Together, the Warrior and the group members hold up their way of life as a model for everyone; their minds are closed, prejudiced against other belief systems or ways of life.

Whenever choices are to be made, or a hierarchy of values established, they will always agree with the philosophy or belief system that the individual holds. The choices are always predictable. This means they are not truly free, open choices. In the dark dance of the Circle of Foxes, the northeast illustrates how individuals are unaware of their lack of free will. They do not know that the choices they make are restricted by the narrow band of possibilities which their core beliefs allow. The tragedy here is that these individuals are convinced that they have free will and that their choices are correct, right, and just. They do not see how predetermined their choices are; they are chasing their own tails. Change and psychological growth are not possible on the Circle of Foxes. The Warrior, for example, will continue to choose the self-reliant, disciplined, rational path, regardless of whether other options are available to him or not.

As the dark dance of life continues, it moves clockwise to the east; on the Circle of Foxes, this is the place of illusion. What is envisioned as a possibility for one's self is limited by everything that has been experienced on the circle. The living of life has been in accordance with the core beliefs framed in childhood. This means that the individual is living up to someone else's expectations of who or what he or she should be. The individual has accepted a role, donned a persona, and is being affirmed by others who share the same philosophy and belief system. Again, there is no awareness on the Circle of Foxes that the dreams and envisionings are illusory. Individuals caught in this dark dance are convinced that they have free will and that they are becoming the persons they are meant to be. If there is any sickness or suffering in their lives, it is usually viewed as something that must be endured. It may even be seen as part of their destiny. The thought that any dis-ease that they experience could be a teaching for them, pointing out where they are not being themselves, is dismissed as nonsense.

The culmination of the life process occurs in the area of self-concepts. On the Circle of Foxes, one's concept of self is defined by the Seven Dark Arrows and as this dark dance is lived, these dark arrows are picked up in the southeast and carried around the circle in an endlessly repeating pattern. The Seven Dark Arrows can influence any or all of the psychological areas outlined on the Circle of Foxes; they also may be shaping the emotional, physical, mental, spiritual, or sexual aspects of one's personality.

The Seven Dark Arrows, defining self-concepts, are these:

1. *Attachments*   This is an inability to see oneself independent of a particular person, place, life-style, philosophy, or whatever. It is a symbiotic merging to the point that the other person, place, or thing defines who one is. The attachment is needed to be one's self and there is no awareness that it is an attachment. In the dark dance, there is always an attachment to one's persona. For example, a beautiful woman who has lived her life being admired and adored for her beauty may not be able to envision life as an old woman. She may feel that without her beauty there is nothing and no reason to live.

2. *Dependencies*   These are less extreme than attachments; there is some awareness of dependencies. Individuals choose to stay dependent out of a fear that they will not be able to stand on their own. For example, a man stays in a relationship that is harmful to him, sacrificing what he really wants to do or be, because he is afraid of being alone. Dependencies cause most of the emotional and spiritual pain in human lives.

3. *Judgments*   A separation between oneself and others occurs when other persons are put down in order to feel good about oneself. The judgment is made using one's own rules and laws, and there is an inability to see any way in which one is like the person or persons being judged. Statements are made like: "I'm glad I'm not like him." Or, "Who would want to be like her."

4. *Comparisons*   An individual, having a strong group identity

and using the collective values of that particular group, criticizes and belittles nongroup members. The group may be religious, political, economic, or whatever, but the individual is absolutely certain that the philosophy and belief system of the group is right. Further, the individual is convinced that what is right for the group is right for everyone else.

(In a Jungian framework, judgments and comparisons describe the projection of the shadow. In judgments, there is the projection of one's personal shadow, the inferior, neglected side of the personality, onto other individuals. What is devalued in one's own personality, is devalued in others. The person doing the judging cannot see and will not admit that the undesirable qualities are within herself. With comparisons, it is the collective shadow of the group that is being projected. The collective shadow may be projected onto single individuals or onto other groups of people.)

5. *Expectations* The rules and laws, and philosophies and belief systems, that govern one's life lead to expectations of how one should act, think, and be. This usually generalizes to expectations of how other people should behave. Very commonly, parents, for example, expect their children to follow in their footsteps, to hold the same values, to strive for the same goals. Expectations are based upon how one thinks things should be.

6. *Needy Child Syndrome* This is the summation of the previous five dark arrows. There is a need to have another person, or several people, around, giving love, acceptance, and support, in order to feel good about oneself. Lacking others, there is little or no sense of self.

7. *Self-Importance* Taking oneself so seriously that one is unable to laugh at oneself and life is the hallmark of self-importance. Caught in self-importance, one is quick to take exception to what people say about one's work, family, friends, beliefs, etc., when what is said is not complimentary. Often it is deep-seated guilt or shame that places one in self-importance. Driven by these feelings, there is a tendency to blame oneself or others continually.

These Seven Dark Arrows may be operating to a greater or lesser degree in any area of one's life. For example, a man could be caught in self-importance and comparisons in the area of religious beliefs and not have these dark arrows operating in his career or workplace. This would mean he could hear criticisms of his work or career but take exception to any criticism of his religious beliefs. Likewise, he would not belittle a coworker for taking a different approach to solve the tasks at hand, but in the religious arena, he would believe that those of other religious faiths do not know the truth and might belittle or criticize them.

The dark dance of the Circle of Foxes is where we all begin as children and where we endlessly circle until we wake up and begin the process of individuation. Adults who are caught in a repeating pattern of behavior, fostered and supported by conscious and unconscious beliefs, have no awareness of the pattern. They are caught on the Circle of Foxes. They have carried into adulthood a pattern begun in childhood, a pattern that prevents them from learning all that it means to be human. The mythologies of childhood with their core beliefs are the fertile ground from which our complexes grow. The experiences of life, in our self-fulfilling prophecies, feed these complexes until they become so strong that the complexes are living our life. We are not. We identify completely with these complexes, and they cement us into our persona.

The Light Dance

The dark dance of the Circle of Foxes is the first movement on the Star Maiden Circle; it is not the only movement. There is also the light dance. It begins with the Dance of the Coyote. Coyote is the trickster, always upsetting the normal, usual, habitual course of events. This is the dance one does when changes begin, comparable to beginning one's path of individuation, becoming conscious of one's complexes and patterns of behavior and realizing that other patterns of behavior are possible. When the changes are completed, the movement on the Star Maiden Circle is called the Walk of the Wolf. It may take more than a lifetime to be at ease on the Walk of the Wolf, for it is as difficult to attain as being an individuated personality.

The Dance of the Coyote and the Walk of the Wolf are not limited to moving in a clockwise fashion, repeating the spiral endlessly. In these movements, one can bridge the circle, dancing from side to side. The influence of the opposite point on the medicine wheel is always taken into consideration. For example, in examining the closed symbols of life experiences in the southwest, one must also include the northeast and consider the choices one makes. In order to experience life fully, new choices are required. When one is caught on the Circle of Foxes, the only choices made are those that maintain the closed symbols established by one's core beliefs. The Dance of the Coyote and the Walk of the Wolf require opening the symbols of life by making choices that are truly free. For examples of closed symbols and closed choices, we only have to look around our society. Many of the people picketing against the motion picture, *The Last Temptation of Christ*, for instance, admitted they had not seen the film nor were they going to. Yet they were convinced the film was sacrilegious and immoral. Their judgments and actions were based upon a closed belief system, free choice was impossible. The opening of closed symbols always requires a change in the choices one makes. And to make free choices, one has to change one's mythology, one's core beliefs. How does our mythology develop? And why do core beliefs have such tremendous influence in our lives?

A closer look at the psychological realities of a small child are warranted here to help understand the power our core beliefs exert on our behavior through the years. It is a fact that human infants and small children cannot survive on their own. In infancy we, as a species, are among the most helpless of all creatures. Without nurturance from another human being, usually the mother, the infant or small child will die. Biologically, in order to survive, we are programmed from birth to bond with a nurturer. For example, a newborn baby first begins to focus her eyes at a distance somewhere between six and twelve inches away. This distance is comparable to the distance between the face of a nursing baby and the face of her mother. This focusing of the eyes is part of the biological program for bonding, and bonding helps assure that the infant will be cared for in a loving way, that the infant will not die.

The biological reality of the infant's helplessness has a psychological concomitant. At its core, the psychological counterpart is a fear of death, of annihilation, of not existing. This fear is rooted deep within the human psyche and usually manifests as a fear of being alone or a fear of abandonment. Anaclitic depression of young children has its roots here, as does the failure-to-survive syndrome in infants. The psychological and the biological processes work together to assure life will continue.

In the development of a core belief, the emotional response that a child experiences most commonly, in fact, almost universally, is the emotion of fear. The child is frightened, and the fear consciously or unconsciously connects to a fear of abandonment and, ultimately, to a fear of death. The fear may be masked by anger, anxiety, or depression. These emotions may continue to be engendered in adult life, covering or disguising the fear of dying, of not existing.

A core belief develops early in childhood and exerts a tremendous influence throughout an individual's lifetime. A little girl, for example, observes her parents anxiously discussing money. Her father is out of work, and there is not enough money to pay the bills. The little girl is frightened. She has never seen her parents so worried before. She doesn't know what's happening. From her frame of reference, she experiences her parents' concern. "Life is hard," she thinks, even if she has not framed the words. "I will have to struggle to survive." She doesn't want to add to her parents' burden. Unconsciously, this is related to the thought: "If they have too many burdens, they won't be able to take care of me." She makes an almost instantaneous decision on how she will act. This little girl decides to be the good, dutiful daughter, rarely complaining of pain or discomfort. Through her youth, she receives affirmation from her parents for her brave, adult ways. As she matures, her core beliefs mold her into a woman her parents admire.

In this example, the little girl's core beliefs typologically have an extraverted focus and, with her concern for others, there is a high feeling component. She grows into a woman who puts herself last. The unexamined childhood fear of abandonment and death now masquerades as a fear of being alone, a fear of being herself. She stays in relationships, denying her own wishes, because she does not want to be by herself. The core belief from her childhood, and her decision not to burden her parents with any of her pain and worries, was conducive to her survival and the survival of the family. As an adult, however, the fear that she cannot stand by herself is anachronistic. It was true in the past, but it is not true now. The fear is so ingrained, however, so much a part of her psyche, that she is unconscious of how influential it continues to be in her life. Her core beliefs, resting on this fear, comprise the myth she has lived out thus far in her lifetime. If she is to move forward, her old mythology must be replaced with a new myth and the old core beliefs with new ones.

The formation of core beliefs are proper and adaptive in childhood. They develop in response to survival needs, whether real or perceived. Yet we need to remember that these core beliefs are formulated by a child's mind. A child's mind cannot handle paradox; it is only capable of focusing on one thing at a time. Further, the child believes that the way she or he is viewing the world, making sense out of it, is identical to how everyone else views the world.

How many of us as children were shocked with the realization that a best friend did not share our deepest beliefs? I remember, as a preteen, wrestling with the realization that we were different — my best friend and I — and I wondered if we could remain friends. Up until then, I had assumed that everyone thought, felt, perceived, and judged in a manner identical to the way I did. Only later, much later, did I learn that struggling with differences is part of the human dilemma and that only with psychological maturity could differences and paradoxes be tolerated. Unfortunately, chronological age has little to do with psychological maturity, so that some elderly human beings may be as incapable of integrating paradoxes as are seven- or eight-year-old children.

The capacity to handle paradox has been examined psychologically under the rubrics of cognitive dissonance and concept development. These studies have revealed that one's belief system is the staunchest deterrent to accepting contradictory facts. For example, in a study involving children of seven, thirteen, and seventeen years of age (Saltz, Dunin-Markiewicz, and Rourke 1975), seven-year-old children were asked: "Are daddies good?" The response was unanimously affirmative. When asked, "Are thieves and robbers good?" the answer was unanimously "No." The seven-year-olds were then asked: "Can thieves be daddies?" Again, a resounding "No." We can smile at this, but what about the belief systems of adults? Studies have shown that they are just as impervious to change.

When John Kennedy was president of the United States, Democrats and Republicans held vastly different images of him and his administration. As the news of his brother Teddy's escapades at Chappaquidick came to light, and later, Jack's bedroom rambles became common knowledge, staunch Democrats were disbelieving of these facts. Republicans, hearing the same information, had no difficulty in accepting the validity of this news. The staunch Democrats who disbelieved the facts were experiencing the same cognitive dissonance as the seven-year-olds who found it inconceivable that thieves could be daddies.

Our core beliefs are powerful, but why do we develop certain core beliefs and not others? Similarly, why do we develop certain cognitive modes in our typology and not others?

Learning theorists would state that we develop our core beliefs or cognitive modes on the basis of positive reinforcement, and the particular selection of a core belief or cognitive mode would probably be described as the product of random chance. There would be an acknowledgment that we have a biological inheritance in our genetic endowment that enables us to be better at some things than at others, and that through trial and error our strengths would emerge. The random selection, trial and error, and positive reinforcement theories are one way of explaining why we develop certain core beliefs and not others. However, the Native American teachings take a different position. These teachings view life as a continuous spiral toward enlightenment. This viewpoint states that we have chosen our lives in order to learn a lesson and that we are born with a predetermined frame of reference that we have chosen. Being born as children into this world, we are not aware of this frame of reference, and, childlike, we believe that our way of functioning, our frame of reference, is universal.

Now let's look more closely at the formation of our core beliefs that constitute our mythology. According to the Native American teachings, the frame of reference you first used when you interacted with the world was one you chose. You chose it in order to learn certain lessons in this lifetime. As a very young child, you witnessed something happening, something you had no control over. Observing the scene from your particular frame of reference, you focused on only one aspect of what was happening. It was impossible for you as a child to focus on more than that one aspect because your mental capabilities were those of a child. You could not comprehend more than one thing at a time. You had an immediate emotional reaction to what was happening. Undoubtedly, you were afraid. After the emotional response, you attempted to understand what you were observing. Being a child, with a child's mental resources and limited by a single perspective, you made sense out of it to the best of your ability. At that instant, the seeds of your core beliefs were sown. From your childish understanding of what was happening, you decided how you were going to behave. Then you began to act in accordance with your core belief. The entire process happens in a very, very short time, probably in milliseconds, and occurs early in childhood, probably at the age of just two or three years. It is firmly ingrained by the time we are six or seven.

What you observed as a child registered in your psyche. It is a psychic truth for you. Someone else observing the scene could have a completely different perspective, but that does not invalidate your perception, your reaction, or your interpretation of the event. How you reacted was the appropriate way for you to behave at that time. Your core beliefs were adaptive in childhood. They provided the structures for your ego defenses which enabled you to survive into adulthood. But now, in order to grow in awareness and move on your path of individuation, it is time "to put away childish things," time to realize that you can become the person you were meant to be, time to move from the myth of your childhood to a myth of your own choosing. Changing your core beliefs is the key to unlocking the trap which has kept you going around and around on the Circle of Foxes.

Core beliefs can be changed. In fact, they do change if you choose to begin the Dance of the Coyote, which would move you onto the light mirror or open symbol dance of the Star Maiden Circle. Because the Coyote is the trickster, you may need to trick yourself and others in order to change your pattern of behavior. The Coyote often looks at things backwards, doing the unexpected, saying the opposite of what was said before. And this gives us a clue as to what the Dance of the Coyote is all about. We may have to consciously shift our perspectives, beliefs, and attitudes 180 degrees in order to break open our habitual pattern of behaviors. But each change we make begins to change the core beliefs we hold about our-

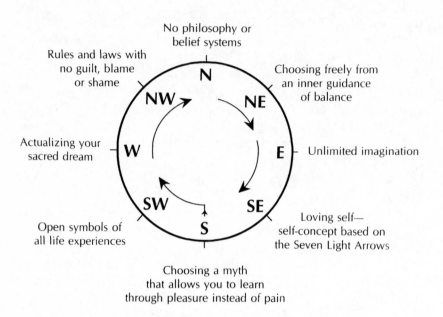

Figure 11. *The Walk of the Wolf Movement of the Star Maiden Circle*

selves. Changes can begin at any point, in philosophies and belief systems, rules and laws, or any other of the eight points on the Star Maiden Circle. All will impact our mythology.

The light mirror dance of the Star Maiden Circle is really the Walk of the Wolf. But we can't move directly to the Walk of the Wolf from the Circle of Foxes. To move onto the Walk of the Wolf, you do the Dance of the Coyote. This dance is not an endless circling going nowhere. With the Dance of the Coyote, you can bridge back and forth across the circle, zigzagging your way around. As we look at the light mirror dance of the Star Maiden Circle, we will look at each point and see its relationship to the point on the opposite side of the circle. When we do this, we will see that there are four pairs, or bridges, that are involved. But first let's see what a completely open, light mirror dance of the Star Maiden Circle would look like.

Beginning in the south, we are again at the place of mythologies and entertainment. But this time, in the light mirror dance, the childish core beliefs which have held us in pain and fear are replaced by the knowledge that we can learn with pleasure and beauty. Childlike, we can be open and curious, living in the moment, congruent with our emotions, laughing when we are happy, crying when we are sad. With new core beliefs, we erase our personal history and move forward to experience life fully, exploring the beauty of living and opening our closed symbols of life experiences. For example, those individuals who picketed *The Last Temptation of Christ* may independently decide: "I can see any movie I want and I want to see them all." As we move to the west, we are actualizing our sacred dreams. We take responsibility for ourselves, claim our own authority to be who we want to be, and live in the present, unlimited by past hurts and unafraid of the future. In the northwest, we have eliminated all guilt, blame, and shame. We live in accordance with sacred law and ignore the social, political, or religious laws that have kept us on the Circle of Foxes. The sacred laws to be mindful of are these:

1. All things are born of woman. This means that the feminine energy in a man or a woman is the creative energy of the universe. Masculine energy is the conceptive energy that carries the image. Feminine energy incarnates the energy, giving it form.
2. Nothing shall be done which will harm the children. This applies to all children, including the child within oneself and others. It also includes the children of Grandmother Earth, so that we would not pollute the water, the earth, or air. We would protect the environment and live in harmony with it.
3. Love is all there is. The energy source of all creation is the spiritual-sexual Eros of the Great Spirit, the Sacred Mystery. We live life in beauty and harmony by loving self, life, and others. Simply stated, God is love.
4. All forms of all things within the everything conform to the Powers of the Four Directions. This is the organizing principle of all creation.
5. All humans are the Trusted Keepers of the Sacred Image of the Great Spirit, therefore honor all humans as your sisters and brothers.
6. Never bring dishonor to yourself, your relations, or your nation by breaking sacred law.
7. All people have the right within the movement of the Great Spirit to follow their own vision. Therefore, never speak critically of your brother's or your sister's dream. Only speak of the dream that dances in your heart. In other words, if you

> haven't walked a thousand miles in the other person's shoes,
> you don't know what baggage that person is carrying.

Following sacred law, there is no guilt, blame, or shame. Each person is seen as doing the best she or he can do. With this approach, our self-concept shifts. Previous life experiences are viewed as a karmic lesson, and once the pattern is recognized, the lesson is learned. It is time for karma to shift into dharma. Limiting complexes are depotentiated. No longer do we blame a parent or anyone else for our problems. We do not say: "I come from a dysfunctional family," or "I am the adult child of an alcoholic," to explain why we are the way we are. We see ourselves as potent human beings, capable of becoming who we are meant to be. We view all human interactions as providing mirrors for us, teaching us something about ourselves.

As we discard the old rules and laws that kept us shackled, we move into the north and determine to have no philosophies or belief systems. We will choose to have minds that are open like an empty cup to receive information. After we have received the information, we will try it, test it in our lives. If it is true for us, we will then know it is true. Knowing, we will incorporate it into our lives, and we will not need a philosophy or a belief system to inform us in what we should believe. No longer will we prejudge, excluding information that is paradoxical. We acknowledge that there are many ways to view the truth, and each way is but one of them.

The choices we make about what we will or will not do are made freely. We are no longer limited by a philosophy or belief system telling us what we should or should not do. Our choices in the northeast are aligned with sacred law, and we accept movement and change as a part of life. We are open to the promptings of our Higher Selves. In Jungian terms, the ego and the Self are in a continuous dialogue. The conscious and unconscious aspects of each personality are dancing together, forming an indivisible unit. Then, with unlimited imagination in the east, we envision the full range of our potential. We no longer feel constrained by needing to please other people or to be what others expect us to be. We are the unique persons we were born to be. The Seven Dark Arrows of self-concept in the southeast of the Star Maiden Circle are replaced by the Seven Light Arrows:

1. *Self-Awareness*   I am willing to look at myself to discover the patterns I have been repeating, to learn and change my childish mythologies.
2. *Self-Appreciation*   I recognize and appreciate the unique being that I am.
3. *Self-Acceptance*   I recognize that, being human, I make mistakes. I will accept the mistakes as teachings.
4. *Self-Pleasure*   I will seek pleasure in everything I do and replace old pain tapes that taught me to doubt myself.
5. *Self-Love*   I will love myself, knowing this is the critical factor in everything I do. The affirmation of my self must come from me.
6. *Self-Actualization*   This is a summary of the previous five light arrows.
7. *Impeccability*   This means always being at cause in my actions. I will hold my true position, never reacting blindly or automatically when someone pushes my buttons. Nor will I imitate the behavior of someone I admire. I will not take myself so seriously that I cannot laugh at myself or life.

The Walk of the Wolf is not attained by making just one change on the Circle of Foxes. There are many, many changes to be made, and they are made by beginning the Dance of the Coyote. These entail bridging from one point on the circle to the opposite side. You can begin this dance with any of the four bridges. Beginning with the south–north bridge, the south is the place of our wounded, needy, little child on the Circle of Foxes who is locked into a mythology of pain and fear. As we begin to free ourself from our childish ways, we allow the little child to become curious, open, trusting, and innocent. We are at one with our emotions, crying when we are sad, laughing when we are happy, and are completely in the present, in the now. As we bridge to the north, we connect with our adult self. It is here that my adult woman, if I am female, or my adult man, if I am male, will have wisdom, without prejudice. With this south–north bridging, the open mind of the adult is balanced by the healed, curious child creating a unique individual who is a harmonious blending of spontaneity and wisdom.

The southwest and northeast points on the circle form a second pair that need to be bridged. When we recognize an experience in life that we have denied ourselves out of fear, we make a decision to experience it. We make our choices and decisions without any limiting prejudices and open ourselves to the pleasure and enjoyment of life. Responding to the inner guidance from our higher self, all closed symbols of life are opened. One's personal dream and sacred dream allows one to give beauty to oneself, life, and others. And as each gives away without any expectations, each is feeding the collective dream of all people. In turn, the collective dream feeds the personal dream.

The west–east bridge connects actualization and imagination. This is the bridge that allows spirit to become substance and substance to become spirit. With unlimited imagination in the east, one envisions what is possible and then actualizes it in the present in the west. The more that is actualized, the more that is imagined, and the energy dances back and forth between these points. One is determining with the spirit and incarnating or holding with the body.

The northwest and southeast points form the fourth bridge. These are the points that connect rules and laws with the concept of self. As the bridge between them is formed on the Dance of Coyote, the dancer discards the guilt, blame, and shame that had molded self-concepts and moves into being a child of the light. With the Seven Light Arrows, we live in accord with sacred law, loving ourselves and knowing that we are loved.

Any change you make begins the process of moving from the Circle of Foxes to the Dance of the Coyote and, ultimately, to the Walk of the Wolf. If you are serious about engaging the dance, then identifying your mythology and the core beliefs that kept you locked into a childish frame of reference is a necessity. Your mythology and core beliefs have become a major part of your persona, defining how you relate to your environment. As you will see, your reliance on particular typological functions is directly related to your mythology and core beliefs.

There are several clues to help you identify your core beliefs and the myth you currently are living. Early memories of our parents sometimes point to what these core beliefs are, since core beliefs began in response to something observed in childhood and often involved our parents. Early memories of any sort may also lead to discovering core beliefs. You can also listen to your internal dialogue and isolate the critical voices you hear. The voices that say: "You can't do it, why try?" or "Someone will see how dumb you are" or "You are not being a good person, you're selfish." You may first hear the voices as voices of someone you know. Your mother, an older brother, or a grandfather, for example. But behind the voice is an archetypal pattern, an inner tyrant, who prefers that you stay unconscious, doing what is expected of you, in fact, living your life for you.

Your fears can also yield clues to your core beliefs. Fears you have now and fears you had in the past. For example, what are the things you told yourself you would never do? What did you believe would happen to you if you did them? Then, what are the things for which you were praised? Often the things for which we were praised are the flip side of our fears.

Because our core beliefs include a particular typological style, an examination of the way we function can be fruitful in pointing out the direction we need to move if we are to break old patterns. In the next chapter, a detailed explanation of how the cognitive modes operate will be given so that you can determine which modes you are using and which you are neglecting.

Chapter 7

A Description of the Cognitive Modes,
Functions, and Orientations in Jung's
Theory of Psychological Types

Definitions

The eight cognitive modes are the building blocks of your personality's cognitive style. The relative strength of these eight modes within your personality determines how you receive and process information to make sense out of your life. Your cognitive style leads you to particular patterns of behaviors. In the descriptions that follow, you will find some cognitive modes that you recognize. These may be very familiar to you, typifying how you function. Others will seem foreign to you and you may find yourself wondering how anyone could function in that manner. "Why would anyone even want to be like that?" you might think, and you may even be glad that you don't function in that way. These unfamiliar cognitive modes are the ones you have failed to develop because they do not align with your core beliefs and your childhood mythology about yourself. You have excluded them from your persona. They do not fit into the ideal image of yourself that you are striving to attain. Nevertheless, the potential for consciously using all eight cognitive modes lies within you. All eight cognitive modes may be developed if you are willing to expand your concept of yourself to include all that a human being can be.

As you read the following descriptions, note particularly those modes which do not describe you. For it is in these neglected, undeveloped aspects of yourself, residing in your shadow, that potential future growth exists.

Jung defined these eight modes and explained how they resulted from the combination of the four functions — sensation, intuition, thinking, and feeling — interacting with the orientations of introversion and extraversion. The four functions exist within the core of each personality as part of our psychological inheritance, but they must combine with extraversion or introversion to be utilized. Sensation, for example, is only in potential form until it is focused outward to perceive the physical world of sights and sounds, or focused inward to perceive the inner, subjective reality. The eight cognitive modes are mental functions, distinct from emotions. They are also distinct from intelligence, will power, or motivation. However, emotions, intelligence, will power, and motivation all interact with our cognitive style in determining our behaviors. It is also important to realize that the eight cognitive modes inherently are separated from neurosis or psychopathology, although an extreme one-sidedness of an orientation or an inferior development of a particular cognitive mode or modes may be symptomatic of mental disorders.

The eight basic cognitive modes are present in every human personality but they are rarely equally well developed and differentiated. Most individuals develop only a few of the eight modes and are unaware of the full potential of their human functioning. All eight cognitive modes are functioning all of the time but the less developed, more rudimentary ones reside in the unconscious and erupt into consciousness only when ego controls are diminished.

The following definitions of the eight cognitive modes differ slightly from the definitions that Jung gave. The research undertaken in the development of the Singer-Loomis Inventory of Personality revealed that the oppositions which Jung presented in his early work on typology do not hold for a great many people. Accordingly, the definitions of the cognitive modes presented here omit any reference to an implied inferior opposite cognitive mode. This means, for example, that in discussing either introverted or extraverted thinking, there is no reference to the feeling function. Therefore, descriptions of inferior value judgments are omitted.

Introverted Sensation

Introverted sensation is the cognitive mode that allows us to be in touch with our kinesthetic and proprioceptive bodily sensations. This mode informs us when we are stressed or relaxed.

If we experience an alpha state of meditation or relaxation, it is through introverted sensation that we know we have achieved this state. We also gain information about our physical state through this mode, for example, we know when endorphins have kicked in, when we reach a runner's high. We may find it almost impossible to convey our experience to others but this does not negate its inner reality.

Individuals in whom introverted sensation is highly developed are attuned to the rhythms of their bodies. They are aware of their high and low energy times in the day, month, or year; they do not need to plot their biorhythms to gain this information. They are sensitive to their bodies and know when something is out of kilter. For example, inner sensations give them warnings which they can heed to prevent becoming acutely ill; they know what foods are energizing for them and which make them heavy and loggy.

With introverted sensation, we are able to see the reality behind the surface and to view life from what Jung called a thousand-year-old perspective. This means that we are allied with a particular, timeless, archetypal viewpoint. It may be that we view the world from the perspective of the victim, or that of the hero, or even that of the long-suffering martyr. Our particular single perspective will color all our behavior if introverted sensation is the most developed cognitive mode in our personality profile. We interact in the world with a bodily sense of knowing who we are.

Extraverted Sensation

With extraverted sensation, individuals connect to the physical aspects of life, to the aromas and tastes, to the visual, tactile, and audible elements of our environment. It is through extraverted sensation that we enjoy or abhor music, sexuality, food, weather, decor. It is extraverted sensation that allows one to note details and to discriminate, for example, a pelican from a swan or burnt toast from hot apple pie, without judging one to be better than the other.

For individuals with highly developed extraverted sensation, the intensity of the experience is what matters, and the sensations of the physical world are brought to an aesthetic level. As a rule, people in whom extraverted sensation is a leading mode will have good memories. Since they record the details accurately, without prejudice, they have no difficulty remembering them accurately. Everyone uses extraverted sensation, but certain aspects may be well developed and others neglected. Unless there is a visual impairment, for example, everyone can discriminate a red traffic light from a green one. But the person in whom the visual aspect in highly developed can discern subtle gradations and combinations of hues. These individuals can match colors from memory; for example, in a paint store, they can distinguish between three or four grey tones and select the one that matches the color of a sofa at home without having a swatch of the fabric with them. Or it may be that hearing is finely developed, and they are able to distinguish pitch and tone in musical scores, or remember and identify the voices of people they haven't heard for years. It is through extraverted sensation that a wine taster is able to identify the region that produced the wine, discriminating a bordeaux from a beaujolais. When individuals have extraverted sensation highly developed in several aspects, they can generally recall a meeting from several weeks or months before, remembering not only what was said and by whom, but often where the participants were seated, what they were wearing, who had on what perfume, and what the pattern and color of the wallpaper was in the room in which the meeting was held.

All interactions in the physical realm are dependent upon the extraverted sensation function. Good extraverted sensation is necessary for people who work with their hands, making things or putting things together. It is a requirement for the seamstress, the machinist, the dentist, and the surgeon. It is also a requirement for an accountant or a chemist or anyone who must be accurate with details and concrete facts. Extraverted sensation keeps our feet on the ground and our mind in the here and now.

Introverted Intuition

Introverted intuition is the cognitive mode that connects us to the unlimited symbols of the unconscious, providing us with a variety of perspectives for viewing life. With introverted intuition, one can switch from viewing life with the timeless perspective of the beggar, to that of the father or the hero, for example, with ease and rapidity. One is not caught in a single perspective.

If introverted intuition is highly developed, the multiple perspectives may be almost simultaneous, enabling the person to see a situation from the perspective of the wounded child and the indignant parent at the same time. Introverted intuition allows us to connect with the endless images of the unconscious and to make inductive leaps, revealing creative connections between ideas or symbols. These leaps "just happen." They are not a product of reason or logic. Introverted intuition is an inward, unfettered imagination, generating ideas and suppositions. It is one of the required modes for philosophers, theoretical physicists, or anyone who is developing a theory. When introverted intuition is highly developed in a visual artist, for example, the images painted on canvas are limitless. For all people, introverted intuition allows life, problems, or situations to be viewed from multiple perspectives.

Extraverted Intuition

Extraverted intuition allows us to see the possibilities inherent in a situation. Extraverted intuition goes beyond what is seen, heard, or perceived in the here and now. When you walk into a room and are aware of the ambience present without noting the specific details of the room, you are using extraverted intuition. Or when you recall the gist of a meeting and the general tenor of what transpired without remembering who said what to whom, you are relying of this cognitive mode. You have a total picture or an overall impression but you are hard pressed to give the details which contributed to your perceptions. Your perception, in these instances, is, as Jung said, a "perception via the unconscious." It is extraverted intuition that gives us our hunches. We don't know where they come from, they just arise.

People in whom extraverted intuition is highly developed are rarely at a loss for speculative or imaginative solutions to a problem. They jump from the present into the future and picture the future as a completed reality without the necessity of considering the systematic step-by-step process by which that final state may be achieved. It might be that you are contemplating decorating an empty room, for example, and the image arises for a specific theme. In your mind's eye, you perceive the room finished. The details remain to be worked out. When extraverted intuition predominates in an individual's psychological makeup, newness and novelty are attractive. These individuals thrive and are energized in situations that provide variety and allow for spontaneity. They are always able to come up with another possibility and are great at speculating. In brainstorming sessions, they are terrific. "Well, what if," they might begin and then go off into another realm.

Introverted Thinking

Introverted thinking is problem solving, which involves concepts, ideas, or symbols. It is primarily concerned with a search for meaning or expanding knowledge. Introverted thinking is the process utilized in the logical manipulation of ideas, as in philosophical reasoning, or the manipulation of abstract symbols, as in mathematics. It is introverted thinking that provides the deductive reasoning utilized in testing hypotheses. In analytic work, when we become aware of a pattern of behavior that is nonproductive, we often use introverted thinking to look back into our personal history to discover the roots of the beliefs and perceptions that produced the behaviors under examination. We may examine parental influences or those of society to shed light on the core beliefs we developed as children, seeking to understand why we are the way we are. In this instance, thinking moves from the present effect (the behaviors in question) backwards, looking into causation. Introverted thinking, moving backwards, is also the function historians utilize to examine our cultural and collective past to determine why our society is the way it is, or why the culture in the United States is different from the culture in Brazil.

People in whom introverted thinking is highly developed often begin problem solving from the position of an inner conviction. For example, in searching for the meaning in one's life or the meaning in society, there is a conviction that an explanation exists. Individuals who rely primarily on introverted thinking work best by themselves. They are primarily concerned with expanding their understanding and knowledge; the meaning of life is of paramount importance. When they present the results of their logical thought processes to others, they can usually communicate the methodical, step-by-step process they have followed. They are primarily concerned with explaining their reasoning and justifying their conclusions. Introverted thinking, when it is highly developed, allows one to remain focused and to carry an idea through to completion.

Extraverted Thinking

Extraverted thinking is the logical problem solving function that connects one to the outer, physical world. It is through extraverted thinking that we have the ability to look at a problem or situation and break it down into its component parts. It is an analytic ability: extraverted thinking allows one to decide the sequence of distinct tasks that need to be done in order to attain a desired goal, determining the sequence on the basis of cause-and-effect relationships.

People in whom extraverted thinking is highly developed determine priorities and hierarchies through logic and reason.

They weigh the pros and cons of possible situations before deciding which solution to choose. Extraverted thinking is a methodical, step-by-step process in which each component is carefully considered. Often this analytic process is done through talking and discussions with others. When extraverted thinking is highly developed, a code of conduct is often developed, and such people may live their lives in accordance with a system of rules and laws that specify what is moral and right. These people can be focused and efficient in getting a job done. Extraverted thinking is a required mode for lawyers, public administrators, or problem solvers in any field. With their task-oriented approach, individuals in whom extraverted thinking is highly developed may appear to others to be cold and heartless.

Introverted Feeling

Introverted feeling connects us to our inner values, to what is written on our hearts. These inner values may or may not conflict with outer societal values, but they are not subject to change with changing times or current trends. Inner values may be personal, developed from your own history, or they may be abstract, such as freedom, deriving from collective history. The values may also be spiritual or mystical.

When introverted feeling predominates in your psychological makeup, you are clear about what you like or dislike. You usually adhere to inner values despite group pressure because you honor what is inside more that what is outside. During the Vietnam war, many young American men refused to enter the armed forces. The collective value in society at that time was "My country, right or wrong." The young men who fled to Canada or openly resisted being drafted were holding personal values that conflicted with the collective. For them, introverted feeling was governing their lives. What they believed to be true was honored despite the pressures of the government, and often the pressures from their family and friends, to change their minds. For those individuals whose behavior is dominated by the introverted feeling function, the old adage "still waters run deep" usually applies, for these individuals are not always open to sharing with others the values they hold dear. In fact, others may view them as stubborn and unresponsive to collective demands.

Extraverted Feeling

Extraverted feeling connects us to other human beings through the ability to share their experiences and recognize their intrinsic value. Extraverted feeling is the necessary ingredient for developing human relationships. It does not have to be the most highly developed mode in both partners, but it must be one of the highest, for true relationships with an enduring intimate quality demand a reciprocity of concern and value for each other. Extraverted feeling always brings the human factor into any decision-making process. This can include the impact of the environment, whether the office or the earth, on the people involved.

When extraverted feeling is dominant, individuals usually adhere to the standards and values of the group to which they belong. They have empathic understanding and a sympathetic ear for those around them. These people are seldom tactless and are usually sought out as confidants because they are easy to talk to. People in whom extraverted feeling is highly developed value other people. They know the appropriate behavior in a given social situation. With another person or in group situations, they may suppress their own needs or desires in order to promote harmony. For them, relationships are of primary importance. They genuinely like other people and have a knack for making others feel important and special.

These eight descriptions describe how the differentiated, well-developed modes function. If, in our cognitive style, all eight modes are differentiated, they interact harmoniously. However, this is an ideal state, and most of us have developed certain cognitive modes and ignored others. Since the cognitive modes do not operate in isolation, but interact with each other, let's look briefly at how the nondifferentiated modes operate.

It is the less-developed modes that are more susceptible to the influence of our emotions and our core beliefs. Selective attention and selective perception come into play when the cognitive modes are in a rudimentary, primitive form. This happens when we see only what we want to see or miss the obvious because it is so contrary to what we want to believe.

Sensation

Sensation is the function that receives information specifying the reality of the inner, subjective world and the outer, physical world. Sensation is the only function that works by itself, and if sensation is poorly developed, it has an effect on all the other cognitive modes.

When introverted sensation is poorly developed, individuals lack a bodily sense of who they are. These individuals may develop eating disorders, becoming overweight or anorexic. They live with stress and anxiety, ignoring the feedback from their inner body mechanisms. Aches and pains are dismissed, and only a catastrophic illness can force them to consider their bodies.

When extraverted sensation is poorly developed, individuals miss the obvious. They ignore facts and details that are right in front of them. They eat to stay alive but have no appreciation for the taste or presentation of the food. The physical environment has little impact on them as they are unaware of their surroundings. They often are unconcerned with how others dress and pay little or no attention to how they look themselves.

Intuition

Intuition relies on imagination. This is the core characteristic of both introverted and extraverted intuition.

When introverted intuition is poorly developed, individuals have difficulty taking different perspectives. There is no validation for another's point of view because another viewpoint just does not exist. They cannot imagine it.

When extraverted intuition is poorly developed, imagination is constricted. The future cannot be envisioned. These individuals are unable to come up with multiple alternative solutions to a problem, and the solutions they do present are often negative, worrisome possibilities.

Thinking

Thinking relies on logic. When poorly developed, both introverted and extraverted thinking processes are illogical.

When introverted thinking is in a primitive, undifferentiated form, individuals are unable to grasp ideas or concepts. They often assign meaning to something that is meaningless, interpreting an innocent gesture or behavior of another, for example, as signifying an ulterior motive or hidden agenda.

When extraverted thinking is undeveloped, individuals see cause-and-effect relationships where none exist. They observe two events occurring sequentially and mistakenly interpret this correlational relationship as one of causation. These people are unable to plan effectively.

Both introverted and extraverted thinking can be erroneous in another way. This is not due to poor thinking or illogical thought processes but due to incorrect data or faulty premises. If the sensation function has not provided the correct information, the resulting logic, although faultless in its process, will result in incorrect conclusions.

Feeling

Feeling is the function concerned with value judgments of liking or disliking, agreeing or disagreeing. All individuals have a standard of values, and judgments rendered are based upon comparing what is being judged to that standard. This is a one-step process, different from the step-by-step process of thinking. When feeling is in a rudimentary form, a good–bad dichotomy exists. Values are black and white.

When introverted feeling is undifferentiated, individuals have difficulty stating what they like. Their inner values are hard to reach and, when found, are in a simplistic, childlike form.

When extraverted feeling is undeveloped, individuals give little or no regard to other people. Sympathy and empathy are absent. Judgments are given in terms of good or bad and people are seen in terms of "If you're not for me, you're against me."

The definitions offered here describe how the eight cognitive modes look when they are well differentiated and how they look when they are in rudimentary form. Of course, there are varying degrees of development between these two extremes. All eight of the cognitive modes exist in your personality. Some you have developed and some you have neglected. From these definitions, you can begin to assess where your strengths and weaknesses lie. You can also use these definitions to discern the specifics of your cognitive style.

There are common patterns of behavior that occur when certain modes are dominant in our personalities. For example, if the four introverted cognitive modes are more developed overall than the four extraverted modes, individuals would have a cognitive style that is globally defined as introverted. But staying only with the label of introverted denies the times when those individuals function in an extraverted manner. Global definitions give a quick picture of the personality. The eight cognitive modes give the details, clarifying the specifics of how human beings function.

In Chapter 3, we looked at how you could begin determining your cognitive style by examining only two dimensions, that of introversion–extraversion and that of perceiving–judging. These two dimensions gave a global view, a quick picture, of how you function. The specifics of how you function can be learned by examining the eight cognitive modes. These will help you determine in which ways you are introverted and in which ways you are extraverted. The definitions will also help you determine which modes you use for perceiving and which modes you rely on for judging.

All eight of the cognitive modes are operating to a greater or lesser degree all of the time. They affect and interact with one another. For a fuller description of the possible interactions, the reader is referred to the *Interpretive Guide for the Singer-Loomis Inventory of Personality* (Singer and Loomis 1984).

Where do you begin if you want to make changes, if you want to develop those neglected parts of your personality? How do you follow and respond to your higher self? This is the topic of the next chapter.

Chapter 8

Correcting the Imbalance

Time for a Change

Noone changes until they become aware that something is wrong, something is out of balance. It may be emotional distress or a physical illness that forces us to realize that we cannot continue living our life as we have in the past. We have to recognize that we have dis-ease in our life before we will change. We have to know that something is out of balance, and we have to know what it is that needs changing. Recognition is re-cognizing, knowing something in a new way. We have to look at our patterns of behavior with new eyes and know them in a new way.

When we examine ourselves with new eyes, we recognize that our persona is identified with our most highly developed cognitive modes while our shadow contains our undeveloped, inferior side. Integrating our shadow, and the inferior cognitive modes that reside there, into our conscious functioning is the first step in restoring the balance. As the shadow is assimilated, our old ego ideal is fractured and a new concept of ourself emerges.

Our new self-image will include what formerly were negative, undeveloped aspects of our personality. We considered them negative and inferior because they did not fit with how we wanted to be seen by others, they did not fit into our persona. By integrating the contents of our shadow, our previous identification with our persona dissolves. We can see the role we have played in society and recognize that there is much more to our being, to our personality, than what was prescribed by the parameters of the old role.

Integrating your unlived side, that part of you that has resided in the shadow, does not cause you to lose what you have already developed. But you may have to curb the overuse of certain cognitive modes. Each of the cognitive modes, in order to function in its optimum manner, must be balanced. Overuse of a cognitive mode prevents the balance from occurring. There is no room, no space for the ignored side to develop. Holding back from automatically acting in old patterns and consciously choosing to behave in a new manner allows room for the transcendent function to emerge. The transcendent function does not emerge immediately, for it is "born of the union of opposites" (Jung 1928, par. 368). It takes repeated efforts at using new behaviors and consciously refraining from falling back into old habitual patterns before the transcendent function is birthed. It is a birthing process, with all the effort and labor that birthing entails.

In the process of individuation, you may often feel as though you are caught in a whirlwind, buffeted on all sides by information, possibilities, emotions. There is an uneasiness and a disorientation. When the transcendent function is birthed, there is a sense of calm, a connection with the core of your personality, a connection to an immutable, eternal center. It is as if you are in the center of a tornado or whirlwind. In the center, in the still point, you can observe the frenetic activity around you, but you are not affected by it. You see the different patterns of behavior that are possible and can choose how you want to be. Regrettably, this feeling does not last forever. But it does occur each time you resolve a particular one-sidedness and move from an either-or position to an inclusive position of both–and. The process of individuation, proceeding by means of the transcendent function results in a "transformation of the personality through the blending and fusion of the noble with the base components, of the differentiated with the inferior functions, of the conscious with the unconscious" (Jung 1928, par. 360).

Where you begin your individuation process is an individual matter. You begin with what your unconscious, your inner higher self, mirrors as a problem of one-sidedness for you. It is an encounter with your own shadow. Often your dreams can point the way if you are able to interpret them properly. But it is not always easy to see one's shadow in dreams, even when one has been trained to do so. It is easier to see your shadow in relationships; in fact, you cannot individuate without relationships (Jung 1951, par. 257).

In our interactions with other people, we are often given emotional clues pointing to what we have neglected in our own personalities. It is through the psychological process of projection that we see in others what we cannot see in ourselves. The clues are given whenever we have strong emotional responses to another person, either extreme irritation or intense infatuation. At such times, we would be wise to determine exactly what personality traits are affecting us. What is it about the other person that either annoys or entices us? After we have identified the trait, we need to examine ourselves honestly, for inevitably it is the same trait or behavior that we have ignored, discounted, or consciously excluded in our own personality.

The trait will always be connected to one of the cognitive modes. For example, say I am bothered by others' indecisiveness, especially by their inability to make a decision when it requires them to state what they would like to do. Am I bothered by such a person because I do not want to be seen as indecisive? Or am I irked because they will not say what they want? My irritation is probably due to the fact that my persona is allied with being decisive and I have not developed my extraverted feeling. An honest self-examination would determine whether I need to develop this cognitive mode. I may need to say what I want and then wait, without acting, without being decisive, until the other responds. Introverted feeling is part of my persona, extraverted feeling is not. The trait irritates me because it does not fit into the ideal image I have of myself, the ideal I am striving to attain. The cognitive mode connected with this behavior (extraverted feeling) has been relegated to my shadow through neglect.

Another way to discover where your one-sidedness exists is to examine the ideal image you hold of yourself. This will lead you to examine your core beliefs and the central myth of your life. Early memories often provide keys to understanding how you adapted to the world of your childhood, how your core beliefs were founded, and to discovering what myth you are living. A woman in her late thirties, for example, remembered seeing her father beating her mother and her mother crying, begging him to stop. She recalled being beaten herself when she voiced what she felt. She quickly learned, as a child, not to cry, not to speak. She learned vigilance to protect herself from her father's irrational rage, for there was no telling what would set him off. She would scrutinize his behavior and then take steps to stay out of his way. Her vigilance required extraverted sensation and extraverted thinking. Her conscious choice not to express what she felt meant she would contain her introverted feeling. This was adaptive behavior, and it allowed her to survive her childhood.

Many women come from dysfunctional family backgrounds similar to the family in the above scenario, but not all are living the same myth. One woman became a warrior, plotting and waiting for the time when she could break free. Knowing what she felt and holding true to her values, she decided that she would never put herself in the position of her mother. She would never be the weeping woman at the mercy of a man. She would keep her silence but only until she could escape. This woman embodies the myth of the Amazon woman and her archetypal core aligned with Artemis. She developed her assertiveness, stating clearly where she was as soon as she was free to do so. This woman never suppressed her introverted feeling. In her childhood, although she was silent, her inner values were the cornerstone of her behavior. As this woman becomes conscious, her task may lie in developing her ability to take another person's point of view, to understand and appreciate where another person is coming from. If so, she might need to develop introverted intuition and extraverted feeling, because these were the cognitive modes, aligned with her myth, that she needed to suppress in her childhood.

Another woman with a similar family pattern but with a different frame of reference became an obedient daughter, falling into the darkness like Persephone. She believed that if she tried harder to please others, especially her father, her life would be different, her father would change. With this belief, she began developing her extraverted feeling and denying her own inner values. Moving into adulthood, living the myth of the obedient daughter, she was disconnected from her own power as a human being, specifically from her power as a woman. She remained unaware of her right to speak of her feelings, to hold her own values. For this woman, introverted feeling did not belong in her persona. For her, changing her core belief from "I don't have a right to like or desire anything so I will be quiet" to "I have the right to my values and the right to say what I like" meant developing the neglected cognitive

Figure 12. Mistakes Wheel

mode of introverted feeling. When this occurs, her old myth of being the obedient daughter will no longer contain her.

When you identify which cognitive modes are aligned with your persona and which are contained in your shadow, you can choose where you want to begin. But be kind to yourself. You are not an automaton that can be reprogrammed by pressing a few buttons. New behaviors will seem strange. You will feel that you are not being authentic with some of them. With others, you may become frustrated at not being as successful as you would like to be or think you should be. Be patient.

There is a Native American teaching, called the mistakes wheel, that is useful when we begin making changes in our patterns of behavior. It is a developmental wheel which you enter in the south, moving first to the north, then west, then east, and ending in the center.

In the south, you give yourself permission to make as many mistakes as you need to make in order to learn the new behaviors. Then you move to the north of the wheel and here you determine to learn from your mistakes. You can make the same mistake three times but no more than three times. Otherwise, you are not learning, and you move from the Dance of the Coyote back onto the Circle of Foxes. You can make different mistakes, but not the same ones over and over. On the mistakes wheel, after you have learned to learn from your mistakes without guilt or shame, you move to the west where you observe and learn from the mistakes of others. You do not have to make the same mistakes that you see someone else making. The fourth step in learning new behaviors places you in the east, where you learn from the mistakes of your teachers. This is a built-in protection to prevent you from falling under the sway of a teacher who may appear to be faultless. All human beings, including teachers, make mistakes. If your teacher does not talk about her or his mistakes, find a new teacher. Finally, the fifth step, the center, is the place where you learn without mistakes.

Most of us demand perfection of ourselves. We can be understanding of someone else's mistakes but supercritical of our own. We want to begin in the middle of the mistakes wheel. We want to learn without making mistakes. This wheel teaches that learning without making mistakes is impossible unless you have already progressed through the other four stages.

Keeping the mistakes wheel in mind, and accepting the reality that you will be making some mistakes, here are some suggestions for developing the neglected cognitive modes.

Introverted Sensation

Pay attention to your body. Discover all that you have held in your body that is outside of your conscious awareness. For example, if you are working on a computer, or engrossed in a task, stop periodically and become aware of any tension you have. Then do something about it — stretch, walk, or exercise. Begin meditating to develop your awareness of what relaxation feels like. Have a massage on a regular basis so that the pleasure of your body can be experienced.

Extraverted Sensation

Ground yourself in the here and now. When you are talking with someone, stay in the present, listen to what is said.

Notice the specifics. For example, when you are walking through a neighborhood, notice the doorways on the houses: see how they differ, attend to the colors. Or you could make it a point to notice the bark on trees and learn to distinguish an elm from an oak by their tree trunks. Listen to music or to songbirds and really hear them. Learn to identify the aromas and tastes of various herbs and spices.

Introverted Intuition

Use figures from your dreams and image them in active imagination so that they become alive and interact with you. Take a perspective 180 degrees opposite from that which you usually hold, for example, relive an argument or discussion from the other person's perspective.

Extraverted Intuition

Follow your hunches. When the telephone rings, guess who is calling before you answer it. Imagine at least three possible solutions to every problem you encounter. Imagine ten or more uses for a common object, like a brick or a paper clip.

Introverted Thinking

Develop your ability to work logically with abstractions. Take a math class, a statistics class, or a course in logic. In any field that interests you—psychology, physics, whatever—memorize the definitions of terms and concepts, then compare and contrast these concepts so that you know how they are similar and in which ways they differ.

Extraverted Thinking

Reach decisions by following a step-by-step methodical process, listing all the pros and cons of each option, then choose the option with the most pros and the fewest cons. Make a list in the evening of what you want to accomplish the next day or the next week, then determine in what order the tasks are to be done so that they will make the most efficient use of your time.

Introverted Feeling

Say what you like. Take on a project — buying new clothes, redecorating a room, rearranging a room — and choose or do only what you like. Do not consult with anyone else for their opinions. Stop giving reasons for your decisions, saying only "I like it." Hold your own space in working with others. Do not acquiesce to group pressure. Do not rearrange your schedule to accommodate others.

Extraverted Feeling

Place the needs of someone else, or a group, above your own wants. Change your plans to accommodate someone else. In arranging a meeting time, for example, yield to what someone else wants. Take time to ask coworkers and family members how they are. Find ways to give sincere compliments and express your appreciation to others for what they do.

You will undoubtedly discover more ways to work on your less developed cognitive modes by observing the behavior of people who irritate you. The first few attempts that you make in using new behaviors will be awkward, and you will probably feel some anxiety. But each time that you use the new behavior, you will gain in ease and grace. And each time you use a new behavior, you are moving off the Circle of Foxes and into the Dance of the Coyote. You are working to birth the transcendent function, which will allow you to use either the new behaviors or the old ones with equal ease. Remember, it is not a sin to make mistakes. Coyote made a lot of them.

Chapter 9

Dreaming a New Myth

There is a myth underlying each of our lives. When we recognize the myth we are living, or the myth that is living through us, we can either choose a new myth or not, but if we do not choose a new myth, we will unconsciously begin living another. The aim of this book is to assist you in dreaming a new myth, seeing yourself as you were created to be, an incarnated aspect of the divine image. As a child, you adopted a myth unconsciously; now, as an adult, it is "time to put away childish things."

In our past, we lived our lives in accordance with how we felt we should be living our lives, how others wanted us to be. In doing so, we forgot who we were. There is story about an old rabbi, named Azusa, who was famous as a wise man and teacher. One day, when his pupils were gathered around him, he spoke to them. "When I was a young man," Azusa told his pupils, "I feared that when I died, God was going to ask me why I was not more like Moses. Now, in my old age, I fear that when I die God will ask me, Why weren't you more like Azusa?"

The path of individuation is, as Jung said, "a way of attaining liberation by one's own efforts and of finding the courage to be oneself" (1958, par. 193). That is the task of this lifetime.

The myth you have been living since childhood is not authentically you. It is an adaptation, an adaptation the wounded, frightened, little child needed to survive. Now it is time to choose a new myth, a myth that will allow you to heal that wounded child, a myth that will allow you to be open, curious, and childlike, but not childish. Having a child's eyes, you can be open to the wonder and beauty and pleasure this world offers, and, at the same time, you can be an adult with mental clarity, using wisdom and logic.

It is time to stop the old tapes that play inside your head, the ones that limit you by saying: "You can't do that" and "Who do you think you are?" It is time to put away the guilt and shame that prevents you from experiencing the fullness of life. There is collective pressure to keep you in your old role, make no mistake about it. As you become conscious and make changes, you affect everyone in your life. The changes you make consciously in your life are like a pebble dropped into a still pool, generating ripples that radiate outward. Your changes force changes in the people around you, and not all of the people in your life will like that.

When I began seriously pursuing my studies in Jungian psychology and my own analytic work, I had to travel out of town. The nearest Jungian analyst was three hundred miles away. On one occasion, one of my daughters complained to me that I would be missing a parent-teacher meeting in which she would be playing the violin. She would be part of the sixth grade orchestra, and she wanted me in attendance. She had every right to expect me to be there. I had been active for years in school affairs, serving as room mother, den mother, whatever, rarely missing a PTA meeting. But this time I said I would not be there. She was disappointed, she was forced to adjust. I had to confront the guilt I felt at disappointing her, at not being a "good" mother. I had to ignore the inner voices that told me I was being selfish.

Sometimes the critical voices in our heads can be identified as parents or teachers, sometimes they cannot. But all of the voices and all of the inner dialogues that induce guilt and shame prevent us from discovering what is written on our hearts, telling us who we truly are. What is written on our hearts was inscribed there by a divine engraver. In the Bible, there is a passage which states that humans do not need to be taught the law by another human being or by a religious authority, for the law is indelibly written within: "Saith the Lord, I will put my law on their inward parts and write it in their hearts" (Jeremiah 31:34). We have forgotten that an inner law, a law without loopholes, overrides any external law. It is a law of love.

This can be a frightening prospect, this idea of obeying the inner law. That there are no loopholes in the law means that I must take responsibility for what I do, for who I am. I can no longer be a child blaming others for my actions. No longer can I point a finger and say, "He made me do it." Or, like Adam, "I didn't take the apple, Eve did." I can no longer duck responsibility. If there is something I do not want to do, for example, I must say, "I do not want to do it," not "My husband won't let me do that." Obeying your inner law means becoming conscious. Becoming conscious means integrating your shadow.

In a Sundance prayer, there is a line which goes like this: "May my shadow fall at my feet always." This image summarizes for me the necessary movement of the individuation process. If my shadow is at my feet, it is as small as it can be. It never completely disappears, yet, if it is at my feet, I am not projecting a long shadow outward onto other people. If my shadow is at my feet, I have integrated most of my personal, neglected potential into consciousness.

The law written on your heart is a law of love. And since the inner and outer worlds mirror each other, love begins with loving yourself. This is a necessary ingredient for consciousness. It is only through self-love that you can "Love your neighbor as yourself." It is only through knowing self-love that you can touch yourself, life, and others with beauty.

Integrating into consciousness the four psychological functions that are manifested as the eight cogitive modes is one of the ways to move toward wholeness, toward knowing, toward loving all that you are. It is taking what was previously neglected, perhaps even despised, and raising it up to a differentiated state.

In a seminar, Jung talked about what the integration of the four functions would be like (Jung 1984, p. 586). He said that with two functions "we have acquired the divine quality of being able to look at ourselves." With three functions, we can observe ourselves, looking at ourselves. And with the acquisition of the fourth function, "that is completion, that is the number 4. That would be the acquisition of the complete divinity of man, namely a complete self-criticism through man himself."

The "complete divinity of man" may seem to be a heretical idea at first. But the realization of the divinity within, the actualization of the *imago dei*, the manifestation of the Self, is what is implied in the psalm "I have said, Ye are Gods, and all of you are children of the most High" (Psalm 82:6). This is what is meant by the Native American teachings that speak of becoming a cell of the Great Spirit's body. The new myth which is waiting to be lived in your life is the myth of being truly free, truly loving, truly divine. It is for you to choose.

It is not to take dominion over the earth or to control another person's destiny that we remember we are gods. As we connect with the divine within ourselves, we recognize and remember the divine within everyone else and the divine that surrounds us. We acknowledge the sacredness of the air we breathe and the water we drink. We respect the ground we walk on and all that grows on the earth. We see our relatedness to the animals, to the stars, and to everything around us.

The Sundance Prayer referred to earlier is a petition, a vow to move in harmony with all things. It is a prayer which brings the "as above" to the "so below" and shows how we as humans relate to everything within the universe. The petitioner speaks as a child addressing grandparents and parents. Quetzyl, Earth Mother, is the spirit of the plants. Coatyl, Earth Father, is the spirit of the animals. This is a prayer appropriate for a new myth.

Sundance Prayer

O – WahKauuan, Sacred Universe, Great Grandmother
O – SsKauuan, Sacred Galaxy, Great Grandfather
Sacred Creatress – Sacred Creator
WakanTanka
O – Great Spirit, Sacred Mystery
Whose voice I hear in the Winds
Walk with me that our hearts become one.
Surround all that is with me with love.
Let my mind become quiet and still as the crystal mountain lakes
Wah! Hey! Sweet precious Quetzyl,
White Buffalo Woman, Earthly Mother
Wah! Hey! Sacred Coatyl, Sweet Medicine, Earthly Father
May my breath flow with the Great Winds and be carried
through the whispering of the trees to join with you.
Let my heart open and soar like the Eagle, O – Wambeidah,
and bring my dance into harmony.
Let my shadow fall at my feet always.

I ask to dance the Acceptance
Circle with all my fellow humans.
I seek to honor the woman and the man
I pledge myself to protect the children
May I walk this Sacred Earth Mother in balance.
O - Sacred Ones
Powers of the Four Directions
WakanTanka - Great Spirit, hear me
I send a voice
This is what I ask
At this time
I have spoken
Ho!

May you dream your new myth, may you dance awake your sacred dream, may you become all you were created to be.

References

Dellas, M., and Gaier, E. I. 1970. Identification of creativity: the individual. *Psychological Bulletin* 70:55–73.

Helson, R. 1971. Women mathematicians and the creative personality. *Journal of Consulting and Clinical Psychology* 36 (2):210–220.

Jung, C. G. 1921. *Psychological Types. CW*, vol. 6. Princeton, N.J.: Princeton University Press, 1971.

―――. 1928. The relations between the ego and the unconscious. In *CW* 7:123–304. Princeton, N.J.: Princeton University Press, 1953.

―――. 1935. The Tavistock lectures. In *CW* 18:5–182. Princeton, N.J.: Princeton University Press, 1976.

―――. 1943. On the psychology of the unconscious. In *CW* 7: 3–121. Princeton, N.J.: Princeton University Press, 1953.

―――. 1951. *Aion. CW*, vol. 9ii. Princeton, N.J.: Princeton University Press, 1959.

―――. 1954. Psychological commentary on *The Tibetan Book of the Great Liberation*. In *CW* 11:475–508. Princeton, N.J.: Princeton University Press, 1969.

―――. 1958. The transcendent function. In *CW* 8:67–91. Princeton, N.J.: Princeton University Press, 1969.

―――. 1984. *Dream Analysis: Notes of the Seminar Given in 1928–1930*. William McGuire, ed. Princeton, N.J.: Princeton University Press.

Loomis, M., and Singer, J. 1980. Testing the bipolar assumption in Jung's typology. *Journal of Analytical Psychology* 25: 351–356.

―――. 1987. An update on the Singer-Loomis Inventory of Personality. In M. A. Mattoon, ed., *The Archetype of Shadow in a Split World: The Tenth International Congress of Analytical Psychology, Berlin*. Einsiedeln, Switzerland: Daimon Verlag, pp. 431–443.

Maddi, S. R. 1976. *Personality Theories: A Comparative Analysis*. Homewood, Ill.: Dorsey Press.

Meier, C. A. 1971. Psychological type and individuation: a plea for a more scientific approach in Jungian psychology. In J. B. Wheelwright, ed., *The Analytic Process*. New York: G. P. Putnam's Sons.

Myers, I. B. 1962. The Myers-Briggs Type Indicator. Palo Alto, Calif.: Consulting Psychologists Press.

Rothenberg, A. 1971. The process of Janusian thinking in creativity. *Archives of General Psychiatry* 24:195-295.

Saltz, E., Dunin-Markiewicz, A., and Rourke, D. 1975. Development of natural language concept: II, developmental changes in attribute structure. *Child Development* 46: 913-921.

Singer, J., and Loomis, M. 1984. *The Singer-Loomis Inventory of Personality (SLIP)*. Palo Alto, Calif.: Consulting Psychologists Press.

Wheelwright, J. B., Wheelwright, J. H., and Buehler, J. A. 1964. *Jungian Type Survey: The Gray-Wheelwrights Test*. San Francisco: San Francisco Society of Jungian Analysts of Northern California.

Zajonc, R. B. 1980. Feeling and thinking: preferences need no inferences. *American Psychologist* 35:151-175.

Index